To Kathy & Terri

This feels like again. We love y company – visit soon.

Love Cathy Ross & Katelyn

July 5/08

D0403078

SCHOTT'S SPORTING GAMING & IDLING MISCELLANY

SCHOTT'S SPORTING GAMING & IDLING MISCELLANY

Conceived, written, and designed by

BEN SCHOTT

BLOOMSBURY

Schott's Sporting, Gaming, & Idling Miscellany™

Copyright © 2005 by Ben Schott

First U.S. Edition 2005

10   9   8   7   6   5   4   3   2   1

Published by Bloomsbury Publishing, New York and London
Distributed to the trade by Holtzbrinck Publishers

All papers used by Bloomsbury Publishing are natural, recyclable products
made from wood grown in well-managed forests. The manufacturing processes
conform to the environmental regulations of the country of origin.

www.miscellanies.info · www.benschott.com

Library of Congress Cataloging-in-Publication Data has been applied for.
ISBN 1-58234-406-X
ISBN-13 978-1-58234-406-5

(Because of expansion in the publishing industry, and the effects of electronic
publishing, the International Standard Book Number [ISBN] is to change.
The existing 10-digit system, introduced in the 1960s, is set to run out of numbers.
So, the International Organization for Standardization [ISO] has ruled that ISBNs
will grow from 10 digits to 13 digits, as from 1 January 2007.)

Designed & typeset by BEN SCHOTT
Printed in the United States of America by
The Maple-Vail Book Manufacturing Group, York, Pennsylvania

SCHOTT'S SPORTING GAMING & IDLING MISCELLANY

A score-card? A rule-book? A handicap certificate? A team-sheet?
A betting-slip? A dance-card? A note from matron?

Schott's Sporting, Gaming, & Idling Miscellany is the third snapper-up of unconsidered trifles. Its purpose is to catch a few loose balls behind the conversational plate. In doing so, the *Miscellany* casts its net wide across the sporting field, gathering in everything from the Noble Art and the Beautiful Game, to the Sport of Kings and the Gentle Craft (see p.140).

But all this frenetic activity is bound to be tiring, certainly for the more sedate gamesters and speculators amongst us. So, alongside field sports, team sports, winter sports, and Olympic sports the armchair athlete will find board games, parlor games, drinking games, and gambling.

And, in pursuit of the complete spectrum of human (in)activity (see p.153), *Schott's Sporting, Gaming, & Idling Miscellany* turns its attention to the ultimate pastimes of indolence, from cards, crosswords, and shadow patterns to bathing, sleeping, and dreaming. Essential reading for idlers, loafers, and *flâneurs* – if they can summon up the energy.

――――――――― VERY DULL ―――――――――

Painstaking efforts have been made to ensure that all of the information contained within the *Miscellany* is correct. However, as Oliver Goldsmith noted, 'a book may be amusing with numerous errors, or it may be very dull without a single absurdity'. The author can accept no responsibility if you get your conker stamped on; catch a chill streaking; shoot a beater; unnecessarily pull in at the pits; raise a royal flush; *fizz* when you should have *buzzed*; or maim yourself horribly somewhere down the Cresta Run.

If you have any suggestions[†], corrections clarifications, or stretching exercises, please email them to usa@miscellanies.info – or send them c/o Bloomsbury Publishing, 175 Fifth Avenue, New York, N.Y. 10010, USA.

[†] The author reserves the right to treat suggestions and exercises as his own, and to use them in future editions, other projects, or to help lend him a lithe and svelte appearance.

The following have been selected for the squad:

Jonathan[s], Judith[g], and Geoffrey[i] Schott.

Richard Album[s], Clare Algar[i], Oscar Anderson[g], Juliet Aston[i],
Stephen Aucutt[g], Joanna Begent[g], Tim Belder[g],
Martin Birchall[g], John Casey[i], Andrew Cock[s], Oliver Cohen[i],
James Coleman[g], Martin Colyer[i], Victoria Cook[i],
Aster Crawshaw[i], Colin Dickerman[i] Rosemary Davidson[i],
Jody Davies[s], Liz Davies[s], Ellie Dorday[i], Will Douglas[g],
Jennifer Epworth[i], Kathleen Farrar[i], Minna Fry[g],
Alona Fryman[i], Penny Gillinson[i], Gaynor Hall[g],
Charlotte Hawes[g], Max Jones[s], David Kamp[i], Robert Klaber[s],
Hugo de Klee[g], Lisa Koenigsberg[g], Alison Lang[g],
Peter Lattman[s], Rachel Law[i], John Lloyd[s], David Loewi[i],
Ruth Logan[i], Chris Lyon[i], Jess Manson[s], Michael Manson[s],
Sarah Marcus[i], Sara Mercurio[s], Susannah McFarlane[i],
Peter McIntyre[i], Colin Midson[s], David Miller[i], Polly Napper[i],
Sarah Norton[g], Mark Owen[s], Cally Poplak[i], Dave Powell[s],
Alexandra Pringle[i], Joel Rose[s], Daniel Rosenthal[s],
Tom Rosenthal[s], Sarah Sands[s], Ian Scaramanga[s],
Carolyne Sibley[g], Rachel Simhon[i], James Spackman[s],
Amy Stanton[s], Claire Starkey[s], Bill Swainson[s],
Matthew Thornley[g], Greg Villepique[i], David Ward[i],
Ann Warnford-Davis[i], William Webb[s], and Caitlin Withey[i].

The full team will be posted up on the board on the day of the match.
Could everyone please ensure that *this* time they have the right kit.

Key to preferred activity: [s]porting · [g]aming · [i]dling

Serious SPORT has nothing to do with fair play
... it is war minus the shooting.

— GEORGE ORWELL (1903–50)

Man is a GAMING animal. He must always be
trying to get the better in something or other.

— CHARLES LAMB (1775–1834)

It is impossible to enjoy IDLING thoroughly
unless one has plenty of work to do.

— JEROME K. JEROME (1859–1927)

---————— DAVE'S OLYMPIC TOP TEN ————---

CBS's *Late Show with David Letterman* celebrated the 2004 Olympics with 'Top Ten Ways to Make the Olympics More Fun', presented from Athens by a decad of American Olympic hopefuls. The suggestions were:

10 · *Gymnasts allowed to smoke during floor exercises* .... Tara Kirk
9 · *Require Dutch track and field team to wear wooden shoes.* . Lindsey Benko
8 · *Replace pommel horse with real horse* .... Rulon Gardner
7 · *Long jump, followed by high jump, followed by wide jump* .... Ali Cox
6 · *Try to make every event a little bit more like Yahtzee* ..... Patricia Miranda
5 · *High dive tank full of sharks* .... Pete Cipollone
4 · *Looser slots at Olympic Village* .... Susan Williams
3 · *Instead of national anthem, play something by Usher* ...... Maurice Greene
2 · *We got badminton — What could be more fun than that?* .. Sarah McMann
1 · *Two words: Nude Fencing* .... Gary Hall

---————— BECKHAM'S BODY ART ————---

David Beckham has, to date, the following tattoos inked upon his body:

Back of neck .... winged cross	Left forearm. *Ut Amem et Foveam*[2]
Lower back .... *Cruz, Brooklyn*	Right forearm .... *VII*
Down spine .... guardian angel	Right forearm. *Perfectio in Spiritu*[3]
Between shoulders .... *Romeo*	Right triceps ...... angel, with text
Left forearm .... *Victoria*[1]	*In the face of adversity*

[1] His wife's name is written in Hindi. Some have rather churlishly pointed out that it may contain a spelling mistake. [2] 'So that I love and cherish'. [3] 'Spiritual perfection'.

BTW — *Mike Tyson has these tattoos:*	Left forearm .... *Monica Turner*
Right triceps .... *Mao Tse-tung*	Face/left eye .... 'tribal' motif
Left triceps .... *Arthur Ashe*	Stomach .... *Che Guevera*

---————— THE 7 DEADLY SINS OF GOLF ————---

Apart from *Missing the Globe* (failing to hit the ball at all) golf's 7 sins are:

Topping .... striking the top of the ball with the bottom of the club
Duffing .... hitting the ground before the ball
Sclaffing .... skidding the club over the grass before it hits the ball
Heeling and *Toeing* ..... hitting the ball with either of the edges of a club
Slicing .... when the ball is sliced to the right by the club
Pulling .... when the ball to the left is hooked by the club

WONDERLAND CROQUET

'Get to your places!' shouted the Queen in a voice of thunder, and people began running about in all directions, tumbling up against each other; however, they got settled down in a minute or two, and the game began. Alice thought she had never seen such a curious croquet-ground in her life; it was all ridges and furrows; the balls were live hedgehogs, the mallets live flamingoes, and the soldiers had to double themselves up and to stand on their hands and feet, to make the arches. The chief difficulty Alice found at first was in managing her flamingo: she succeeded in getting its body tucked away, comfortably enough, under her arm, with its legs hanging down, but generally, just as she

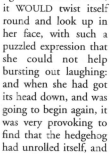

had got its neck nicely straightened out, and was going to give the hedgehog a blow with its head, it WOULD twist itself round and look up in her face, with such a puzzled expression that she could not help bursting out laughing: and when she had got its head down, and was going to begin again, it was very provoking to find that the hedgehog had unrolled itself, and was in the act of crawling away: besides all this, there was generally a ridge or furrow in the way wherever she wanted to send the hedgehog to, and, as the doubled-up soldiers were always getting up and walking off to other parts of the ground, Alice soon came to the conclusion that it was a very difficult game indeed.

— LEWIS CARROLL, *Alice's Adventures in Wonderland*, 1865
[illustration by Sir John Tenniel]

SNOOKER BALL VALUES

Red	1	Brown	4	Black	7
Yellow	2	Blue	5	Orange†	8
Green	3	Pink	6	Purple†	10

† These two balls were introduced into a variant of the standard game called Snooker Plus – devised by the world snooker and billiard champion Joe Davis in response to fears that the popularity of snooker was in decline. Davis proposed that a purple ball be placed between brown and blue, and an orange ball between blue and pink, in the hope that this would encourage break building. The addition of these two colors meant that the maximum possible break increased from 147‡ to 210. Snooker Plus was introduced to the public in October 1959 during a *News of the World* tournament, but never really took off.
‡ It is possible to have a break of 155 assuming that it starts with a free-ball red and black.

———————— THE TRIPLE CROWN ————————

To win the Triple Crown a horse must win three of the greatest challenges in racing at three different tracks, in three different states, over five weeks:

KENTUCKY DERBY	PREAKNESS STAKES	BELMONT STAKES
Churchill Downs	Pimlico	Belmont Park
Louisville, KY	Baltimore, MD	Elmont, NY
distance 1¼ miles	*distance* 1³⁄16 miles	*distance* 1½ miles
record time 1:59⅖	*record time* 1:53⅖	*record time* 2:24
(Secretariat, '73)	(Louis Quatorze, '96	(Secretariat, '73)
	Tank's Prospect, '85)	
purse $1m*	*purse* $1m*	*purse* $1m*

Although, to date, 18 horses have won the first two legs of the Triple Crown, since the inception of the challenge, only 11 have won all three.

year	*horse* (jockey)		
'78 . . . . Affirmed (Steve Cauthen)	'43 . . . . . Count Fleet (John Longden)
'77 . . . . . . Seattle Slew (Jean Cruguet)	'41 . . . . Whirlaway (Eddie Arcaro)
'73 . . . . Secretariat (Ron Turcotte)	'37 War Admiral (Charles Kurtsinger)
'48 . . . . Citation (Eddie Arcaro)	'35 . . . . Omaha (Willie Saunders)
'46 . . . . Assault (Warren Mehrtens)	'30 . . . . Gallant Fox (Earl Sande)
	'19 . . . . Sir Barton (Johnny Loftus)

* Currently, Visa USA sponsor a $5m bonus prize for the owner of any Triple Crown winner.

———————— CRICKETING DUCKS ————————

In cricketing terminology, batsmen are out for a 'duck' when they are bowled out having scored no runs. It seems the term derives from the shape of the number zero which, when written on the score-card, was said to resemble a duck's egg. From this, a range of other terms has evolved:

DUCK. . . . . given out without having scored a single run
A PAIR (OF SPECTACLES). . . . . ducks in both innings of a match
GOLDEN DUCK. . . . . given out on one's first ball
A KING PAIR . . . . golden ducks in both innings of a match
SILVER DUCK† . . . . given out on the second ball of match
DIAMOND DUCK† . . . . given out on the first ball of a match (?)
PLATINUM DUCK† . . . . given out on the first ball of a season (?)

† Entries marked thus are at best tentative and at worst utterly spurious. · The Primary Club is a cricketing charity founded in 1955 to support sporting and recreational facilities for the visually impaired. Membership in the club is open to all, but especially welcome are those who have been given out first-ball at any level of the game.

POKER ANTES vs BLINDS

ANTES are set amounts that every player must contribute into the pot before the start of each hand. The sum does not count towards any future bet and is a sort of 'payment to play' that makes even low-action hands worthwhile. BLINDS are sums, based on the the limit of the game, paid by two players each hand. The player to the left of the dealer (or the symbolic dealer's button) pays the BIG BLIND, and the player two to the left pays the SMALL BLIND. The big blind puts in a sum equal to the small limit ($5 in a $5/$10 game); the small blind puts in half this sum. Unlike antes, blinds *do* count towards the first round of betting – so, for example, in Texas Hold 'Em, if the pot is not raised pre-flop, the small blind will only have to double his blind to match and call the big blind.

SQUASH BALL COLORINGS

Squash balls (whatever their overall color) are usually coded with a colored dot which indicates how fast they will travel. As a general rule of thumb, better players will use slower balls, and amateurs faster ones:

Super slow .. (Double) Yellow Dot	Medium .... Red Dot
Slow......... White or Green Dot	Fast. .. .. Blue Dot

THE MARATHON

In 490BC, the Greek soldier Pheidippides[†] ran from Marathon to Athens, a distance said to be around 23 miles, to break to the Athenians the news that the Persians had been defeated in battle. After imparting his message, Pheidippides dropped stone dead. At the first modern Olympic Games in Athens (1896), a race was held of approximately the same length to commemorate Pheidippides' run, and the marathon was born. At the first few Olympics the marathon was run over 26 miles. At the 'suggestion' of Queen Alexandra (consort to Edward VII) the marathon at the 1908 London Olympics was extended by 385 yards so that it started on the lawn of Windsor Castle on its way to the Olympic stadium in White City. This allowed Princess Mary and her children to watch the start from the nursery window. To this day some of the more sarcastic marathon runners shout 'God Save the Queen' as they pass the 26-mile mark. In 1924 this arbitrary distance became the standard length of a marathon.

[†] There is some debate as to whether it was actually Pheidippides who made this famous journey. It seems likely that it was Pheidippides who ran the 150 miles from Athens to Sparta to enlist support *before* the battle. However, opinion is divided as to whether he or an unknown courier made the fatal run back from Marathon.

SWITCHING SIDES

Notable athletes who, for whatever reasons, have switched national sides:

name [event]	from	to
Saif Saeed Shaheen† [steeplechase]	Kenya	Qatar
Eunice Barber [heptathlon]	Sierra Leone	France
Lennox Lewis [boxing]	Canada‡	Great Britain
Zola Budd [3000m]	South Africa	Great Britain
Wilson Kipketer [800m]	Kenya	Denmark
Fiona May [long jump]	Great Britain	Italy
Greg Rusedski [tennis]	Canada	Great Britain
Ludmilla Engquist [100m hurdles]	Russia	Sweden

† Formally Stephen Chirono, he changed his name to represent Qatar, and secured $1m for the switch. ‡ Lewis won Gold for Canada at Seoul but then switched to Great Britain.

NINE MEN'S MORRIS · MERELLES

Merelles is an ancient game, played either on a board or cut into grass:

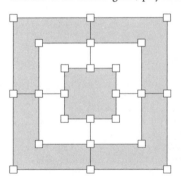

In turn, players lay 1 of their 9 men on the board's intersecting points: the aim is to get 3 men in a row (a MILL). When a player makes a MILL they can remove 1 of their opponent's men from the board (so long as it is not part of a MILL and there are other available men). Once all the men are down, they can be moved along lines to adjacent points. The game ends when a player has only 2 men, or when a player can't make a move.

A REMEDY FOR IDLENESS

'It has been advised for a fit of idleness, to sit down and count the ticking of a clock for one hour, and the individual will be thankful to get up and work like a native, rather than spend another hour in the same manner.'

— ANONYMOUS, *Advice to the million by a friend to the people*, or
How to live and enjoy sound vigorous health on sixpence per day, *c.*1830

—————————— THE POOHSTICKS BRIDGE ——————————

The game of Poohsticks was introduced to the world in A.A. Milne's classic *The House at Pooh Corner* (1928). The game involves dropping a number of sticks over one side of a bridge and seeing which emerges first on the other. It is generally considered to be a Very Relaxing Game. The bridge upon which Milne and his son Christopher played Poohsticks is located in Ashdown Forest in East Sussex; it was built in 1907 by John C. Osman, and was originally known as Posingford Bridge. The architectural diagram below shows both plan and elevation of the original Poohsticks Bridge – as well as suggesting an ideal 'Racing Line' for Poohsticks:

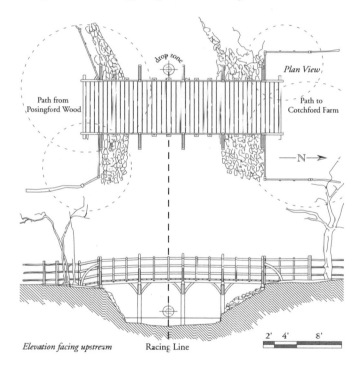

Field research indicates that adopting the Racing Line illustrated above can reduce a stick's time by up to 5 seconds. Clearly, the Racing Line will be influenced by a range of seasonal conditions including weather, water flow, and atmospheric pressure, as well as assorted flotsam and jetsam.

——————————— DATING & THE BASES ———————————

Below are the traditional 'dating bases' with one version of their meaning:

1st base............ *kissing; necking*	3rd base .... *'below the waist'*
2nd base.......... *'above the waist'*	Home plate .... *'all the way'*

However, recent observation of youthful sexual proclivities suggests that inflation may have crept into the standard 'baseball' analysis of dating, with 3rd base replacing 2nd, and now including oral sex. Indeed, as the esteemed social commentator Tom Wolfe notes in his insightful book *Hooking Up* (2000): 'Today first base is deep kissing, now known as tonsil hockey, plus groping and fondling this and that. Second base is oral sex. Third base is going all the way. Home plate is being introduced by name.'

A version popular in the parts of England delineates the five bases thus: [1] Kissyface · [2] Upstairs-Outside · [3] Upstairs-Inside · [4] Downstairs-Outside · [5] Downstairs-Inside. Readers in search of further information should refer to *Paradise by the Dashboard Light* (Steinman / Meat Loaf).

——————— ON THE CLASSIFICATION OF DOODLES ———————

Doodles are sketches or scribbles drawn while the attention of the conscious mind is elsewhere. Sadly, little research appears to have been undertaken into this fascinating field of human idleness. However, in 1938 Dr W.S. Maclay et al. [*Proc Roy Soc Med* 1938; 31:1337–50] undertook an analysis of 9,000 doodles that had been sent in to a newspaper by its readers. (The paper promised to have the doodles analyzed by an 'expert psychologist', and to award prizes.) Maclay classified the doodles thus:

type	composition	%
Scenes......	*resembling an ordinary representation of a subject*	11
Medley	*stray, well spaced, items, independent of each other*	38
Mixture.....	*independent items, overlapping or intermingling*	32
Scribbles	*unelaborate lines or scrawls*	7
Ornaments	*stylized decorative patterns*	12

Within each of these groups, the doodles were categorized by how many of the following features they contained: Stereotypy [endless repetition], 30%; Ornamental detail, 60%; Figures, 38%; Animals, 35%; Objects, 55%; Faces, 60%; Movement, 16%; Numbers, 37%; and Writing, 60%.

Some Australian restaurants in the 1930s provided menus with extra white space to encourage diners to doodle upon the cards rather than their tablecloths. *Doodling* is also an old term for playing the bagpipes, which were known as 'doodle-sacks'.

―――――――― THE WACKY RACES ――――――――

In Hanna-Barbera's cartoon series *The Wacky Races,* 11 teams competed for the title of the 'World's Wackiest Racer' – no doubt inspired by Blake Edwards's 1966 film *The Great Race.* The wacky vehicles and drivers were:

No.	Vehicle	Drivers
00	The Mean Machine	Dick Dastardly and Muttley
01	The Bouldermobile	The Slag Brothers: Rock & Gravel
02	The Creepy Coupe	The Gruesome Twosome
03	The Ring-a-Ding Convert-a-Car	Professor Pat Pending
04	The Crimson Haybailer	The Red Max
05	The Compact Pussycat	Penelope Pitstop
06	The Army Surplus Special	The Sarge and Private Meekly
07	The Bullet Proof Bomb	The Ant Hill Mob[†]
08	The Arkansas Chug-a-Bug	Luke & Blubber Bear
09	The Turbo Terrific	Peter Perfect
10	The Buzzwagon	Rufus Ruffcut and Sawtooth

† The Ant Hill Mob (voiced entirely by Mel Blanc) was comprised of Clyde, Zippy, Softy, Ding-a-Ling, Pockets, Snoozy, and Yak-Yak. A somewhat reconfigured Ant Hill Mob appeared in a spin-off cartoon series, *The Perils of Penelope Pitstop*, driving Chugga-Boom.

―――――――― THE JOY OF BACKGAMMON ――――――――

Backgammon has always been a fire-side, a domestic, a conjugal game; it is not so abstruse as to banish conversation on general topics; it does not, like chess, or love, or art, or science, require the entire man, whilst the ever-recurring rattle of the dice keeps the ear alert and the attention alive; it has often been found an anodyne to the gout, the rheumatism, the azure devils, or the 'yellow spleen'.

— GEORGE FREDERICK PARDON, *Backgammon,* 1844

―――――――― ON WOMEN PLAYING TENNIS ――――――――

WILFRED BADDELEY · 1895
'If a lady intends to play lawn tennis, the first thing she must make up her mind to do is run about, and not merely take those balls that come straight to her, giving up the others as too difficult.'

RICHARD KRAJICEK · 1992
'80% of the women playing at Wimbledon are lazy, fat pigs and shouldn't be allowed on the show courts.' (The next day Krajicek clarified his position: 'I said 80% of the top 100 are far pigs but I just over-exaggerated a little bit. What I meant was only 75%.')

THE PAMPLONA BULL RUN

Pamplona is the ancient Basque city in northern Spain famed for the annual 'running of the bulls', which takes place 7–14 July as part of the festival celebrating St Fermin – the city's patron saint. The purpose of the run is to transfer to the bullring each morning the six bulls which will fight that afternoon. For centuries, hundreds of foolhardy folk have dared to run along the narrow streets in front of the bulls – the aim being to see how close one can get to the animals without being trampled or gored to death. Runners must enter the fenced area of the run by 7·30am, after which they sing a song three times – at 7·55am, 7·57am, and 7·59am:

A San Fermín pedimos, por ser nuestro patrón, nos guíe en el encierro, dándonos su bendición	*We ask for San Fermin, who is our Patron, to guide us through the Bull Run, and give us his blessing.*

Then, at precisely 8·00am a rocket is launched to announce that the gates of the *Santo Domingo* enclosure [A] are open; a second rocket indicates that all the bulls have left the enclosure and are running down *Santo Domingo* [B] towards the the *Plaza Consistorial* [C]. A sharp turn takes the bulls up *Mercaderes* towards [D] where they turn into the long and narrow *Estafeta*. The bulls tend to slow down along this section until they exit the street [E], and enter the fenced funnel, *Teléfonica* [F], which herds them up the narrow *Callejón* [G] and into the *Plaza de Toros* [H]. A third rocket indicates all the bulls have entered the bullring, and a final rocket is fired when the event is over. The 825m run lasts, on average, just 4 minutes.

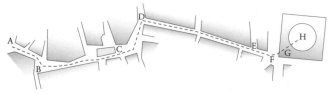

The popularity of the bull run is hard to fathom, especially since injury and death are not uncommon. The city of Pamplona advises that 'runners need to be calm people with good reflexes and in excellent physical shape' – though since 1910 at least thirteen have been killed during the run.

CHECKMATE

The term *checkmate*, used in chess to describe the position where a King cannot escape from an attack, literally means 'your King is dead' and it derives from the Arabic (and Persian) words *shah* (king) and *mat* (dead).

——————————— WALKING DEFINED ———————————

The definition of walking for the purposes of racing is set down by the International Association of Athletic Federations (IAAF) in Rule 230.1:

Race Walking is a progression of steps so taken that the walker makes contact with the ground, so that no visible (to the human eye) loss of contact occurs. The advancing leg shall be straightened (i.e. not bent at the knee) from the moment of first contact with the ground until the vertical upright position.

Given the difficulty of maintaining these strict requirements over a long distance, disqualifications are not uncommon. For example, at the 2000 Sydney Olympics, Janet Saville was 150m away from a gold medal in the 20km walk when an Italian official issued her with a red card for 'lifting'.

————————— GOLF STROKE NOMENCLATURE —————————

Ace	hole in one	Par	0
Deuce	hole in two	Birdie	-1
Double Bogey	+2	Eagle	-2
Bogey	+1	Double Eagle, Albatross	-3

Until the 1940s or so, the term *Bogey* was used in the same way as *Par*, i.e., the 'scratch' number, or the number of strokes a good player ought to take on a hole. (Curiously, this number used also to be known as The Colonel, after a fictional military type who 'laid down the law'). Later, perhaps because of American influence, *Bogey* came to mean a stroke over Par. The Par of a hole usually depends on its length: usually Par 3, <250yds; Par 4, 251–475yds; Par 5, >476yds. The etymology of *Birdie* is a little unclear, though it might derive from old American slang where a 'bird' was anything pure, exceptional, or smart. It can safely be assumed that the use of *Eagle* and *Albatross* came about simply because they were more impressive birds. (Some players highlight Birdies on their scorecard with a circle, and Eagles with a square.) In the C19th, another set of terms was used to describe the number of strokes one had taken in relation to one's adversary. If your opponent had played one stroke more than you – known as 'the odds' – your next stroke would be 'the like'; if they had played two strokes more – that is, 'the two more' – your next stroke would be 'the one off two'; if three more, 'the one off three', and so on. One definition of a golfer is someone who shoots a five, shouts *Fore!*, and cards a three.

——————————— ALL-AROUND ATHLETICS ———————————

The *all-around athletics contest* (which ran *c.*1884–1976) was a forerunner of the decathlon. The following nine events were contested in one day:

100yd dash · mile run · 880yd walk · 120yd hurdles · high jump
broad jump · hammer throw · pole vault · 56lb weight throw

——— SOME PARLOR GAMES ———

The game of HESTIA involves two of a party secretly agreeing on a word which has various meanings, and then discussing the word in conversation in its various forms. Other members of the group may only join in when they think they have figured out the mystery word. For example, the word 'hare' might be talked about in the following way: 'Does yours run very fast?' 'No, but it grows quickly.' 'Is it brown?' 'Surely you can see that it is going gray!' – and so on until all but one player has twigged. The variant NEW HESTIA sees the word agreed by all of the group except one player who must guess from listening to the banter.

The timeless game of mental mathematical agility FIZZ BUZZ demands that all the players take turns in counting up from 1, substituting the word *fizz* for any multiple of 3, and *buzz* for any multiple of 5. If a number is a multiple of both 3 and 5 then *fizz buzz* is called. So, counting would start: '1, 2, *fizz*, 4, *buzz, fizz*, 7, 8, *fizz, buzz*, 11, *fizz*, 13, 14, *fizz buzz*, 16…' and so on. Of course, after this things get a little tricky.

The game of DUMB CRAMBO involves each player acting out a series of words which rhyme with the word they have been set, until that word is guessed by the rest of their team. For example, a player set the word 'tie' might act out the words 'die', 'spy', 'fly', 'fry', and so on, until 'tie' is correctly guessed.

The invention of the Post-it note has greatly facilitated the playing of FOREHEAD DETECTIVE. Here, each member of a group is allocated a famous character by the person on their left who writes the name on a piece of paper and appends it to the victim's forehead so that while they cannot see the name, it is visible to the rest of the group. Each player then takes it in turn to ask yes/no questions about their character until they are able to identify them.

In the lovely word-game LONDON UNDERGROUND players take it in turn to describe stations on the London tube network for other players to decode, for example:

Fabricated from beer…	Maida Vale
Vicar's envy………	Parsons Green
Burnt BBQ…………	Blackfriars
Additional heath…….	Moor Park
Let pig decay……	Turnham Green
Fill up a shop…………	Stockwell
Larger lair for thieves……	Morden

(Of course, this game can be played with any underground network or, indeed, any mutually agreed geography. For example, Times Square might be 'obloid watch'…)

The SIMMONDS'S CAT is just one of many alphabet games. Players take it in turn to name an adjective to describe the Simmonds's cat – the initial letter of the adjective rotates through the alphabet. 'The Simmonds's cat is an *artful* cat'; '… a *belligerent* cat'; '… a *cheerful* cat'. A requirement for speed can be introduced into the game for more competitive players.

In the game ADVERBS, while one player has left the room, each of the others selects their own adverb (e.g. *stupidly, clumsily, cheerfully*). The excluded player asks each person to perform an action (e.g. tying a shoelace, reading from a newspaper, &c.) in the manner of their adverb. The excluded player is allowed 3 guesses at each adverb.

At the start of the spelling game GHOSTS each player has 3 lives. The first player proposes a letter to which each subsequent player (in turn) has to add another letter. Any player who, by adding a letter, completes a word (longer than 3 letters) loses a life. Any player who is challenged and cannot propose a legitimate word they were 'aiming for', loses a life. Any player who makes a challenge which is shown to be unfounded loses a life. When a player has lost all of their lives they become a 'ghost', unable to propose letters, but able to harry and make misleading suggestions. If a ghost succeeds in tricking another player into losing a life. they are then reconstituted into living players of the game. Expert players who tire of the basic game can play REVERSE GHOSTS where words are spelled backwards.

REVERSE BOTTLETOP SPILLIKINS is played with a box of matches and a wine bottle. Players take it in turn to balance a match on the top of the wine bottle – the player who disturbs any of the matches so that it falls is deemed the loser.

The game WHAT'S WRONG? is a simple test of observation. All players but one are sent out of a room and, in their absence, a number of changes are made to the room's organization (e.g. the clock is advanced an hour; a picture is moved or replaced, &c.). After a few minutes the others in the party return and have to write down what they think has been changed. Whomsoever identifies the most changes made to the room wins.

A number of parlor games can be played with a feather. FEATHER FLIGHT involves trying to keep a feather aloft by blowing – anyone who touches the feather is out. FEATHER FOOTBALL requires two teams on either side of a table. The aim is to blow the feather into the other team's half so that it touches either an opposing player, or so that it falls on the opposition's side of the table.

CHARACTER ASSASSINATION is best played with a group of close friends or relatives. With one person out of the room, the remaining players swap identities with one another. The excluded player must identify who is who by posing a set of questions or setting a series of tasks. The game may be expanded by including characters who are not actually present but are familiar to all.

[For a selection of forfeits which may be employed with these games, turn to p.136. For the ultimate parlor game, see the alleged death of Palmerston on p.42.]

TIPS FOR CONJURORS

Advice from *The Magician's Handbook* (1902) by 'Selbit' – a pseudonym of Percy Thomas Tibbles – who petulantly warns: '[if these] rules are not attended to, do not forget that you were well advised to remember them.'

1. When you enter the drawing room to do your show, do not go round and shake hands with the company. This might be taken for a piece of undue familiarity.

2. Do not say that if a trick is not properly applauded you will not continue your show. This would be considered a little out of place.

3. Presuming that you are doing a card trick and that a lady will not select the card you are attempting to force, do not swear at her. Swearing is not considered polite in Society.

4. When a bald-headed gentleman resents your producing eggs and cigars from his pate, do not tell him to keep his hair on.

5. If you bungle a trick and the audience notice it, do not explain the mistake by saying that you must be a fool. Possibly they might fall in with your belief.

6. Do not call the parlour-maid pet names or engage her in conversation to the neglect of your hostess. Remember that you are getting a free meal and that it is your duty to listen to ladies talking.

SOME CARD-SHARP SLANG

Mark; Bozo; Beezark; Umpchay	the target of a scam
Broad tossers	three-card monte operators (see p.95)
Hustle the duke	work the trains
Hustle the big drink	work ocean liners
Bloomer	bad or unprofitable play
Paperman	gambler who marks cards
Mechanic	expert card manipulator
Beetle-proof	victim who is not bamboozled by female charms
Duke the money	get to know the mark
Cannon; Dip	pickpocket
Poke	wallet
Pasteboard	card-table
Tossing the cop	letting the mark win
Take the uffy-duffy	to keep, and not regamble, winnings
Mr Hemingway	traditional *nom de guerre* for a card-sharp
Greek-bottom	dealing the second card from the bottom of a pack

Extracted from Michael McDougall's classic *Gamblers Don't Gamble*, 1939. See also p.105

──────────── THE LANGUAGE OF FALCONRY ────────────

Falconry is the art of training and employing birds of prey – falcons or hawks – in the service of man. It seems that China knew falconry as far back as 2000BC (the Chinese even hunted butterflies with hawks), and Japan knew the sport around 600BC. From these civilizations, and the trade routes they developed, falconry traveled West, where it was embraced by the Mongols, Persians, and Arabs before sweeping across Europe. Although under English law (e.g. the Forest Charter of 1217) any free man could own a hawk, from its arrival in Britain falconry was considered a noble, aristocratic, and essentially regal activity. (This was in part guaranteed by the cost of the birds, the elaborate diet they were fed, and the extensive training they required.) Falcons were exchanged as gifts by monarchs, and were even considered to be appropriate exchanges for aristocratic prisoners of war. Kings in succession framed legislation to protect their rights to keep and hunt with hawks – under Edward III the stealing of a hawk became punishable by death. The class distinction of falconry embraced not only which type of hawk might be owned by which rank of individual (see p.118), but also the complex vocabulary which hawksmen employed. As Ben Jonson wrote, 'to speak the hawking language was affected by the "newer man" who aped the manners of the older gentry'. Some of falconry's poetic terms are translated below:

Hawks do not breed but *eyer*, and are not hatched but *disclosed*. Hawks are *reclaimed* not tamed, and they are not trained but *made* or *manned*. Hawks do not chase animals, they *fly after fur*, *after feather*, or *after plume* and, when they have sighted their prey, hawks do not swoop but *stoop* to attack the *inke* (neck) of their quarry. Once killed that quarry becomes a *pelt*, not to digest but to *endew* especially if the hawk is hungry or *sharp set*. After a meal hawks do not preen themselves but *rejoice* and they do not clean their beaks, rather they *freak* them. Such a distinguished creature would never molt, instead they *mew*[†]. Hawks do not perch but *take stand*; they do not drink but *bowse*; they do not sleep but *jenk*; they *bate* rather than beat their wings; and do not shake their feathers, rather they *rouse* them. They do not fight with other birds, rather they *crab*. A hawk is never fat or overweight, but *high* and, when high, will be *enseamea* to purge excess weight. A hawk is never constipated, but suffers from *craye*, and does not cough but *keck*. Of course, hawks are never actually ill – rather they are said to suffer from *ungladness*.

[†] We derive 'mews' from the buildings where hawks were kept while they molted (or mewd) – *mew* comes from the Latin *mutare*, 'to change'. Our current use of mews to describe where horses are stabled dates back to 1534 when the Royal Mews in Charing Cross, London – originally the home of the King's hawks – were given over to horses.

———— 'COOTIE CATCHER' FOLDING ————

 1   2   3

Take a square sheet of paper, and fold each corner in half to mark the center[1]. Fold each corner into the center [2] to form a smaller square and turn the paper over [3].

 4   5   6

Fold each corner into the center [4] and crease the square across its center (vertically and horizontally) [5]. Fold the paper in half and turn it over [6]. Tuck your thumbs and first fingers under the four square flaps [7] and push upwards and outwards.

 7

Under the innermost flaps scribble a set of appropriate predictions ('you fancy Miss Thomas'); annotate the inside flaps with numbers; and decorate the outside flaps with colors. Ask the victim to pick a color from the outer flap and, with your fingers under the flaps (as in 7), open and close the folder, vertically and horizontally in turn, once for each letter in the color chosen. Then, with the folder open at the appropriate place, ask the victim to pick one of the visible numbers. Open and close the folder as many times as the number picked. Ask the victim to choose another of the visible numbers; lift the corresponding flap and reveal their future.

———————— MEXICAN WAVES ————————

Although 'Mexican waves' – the undulating effect of a crowd of spectators jumping to their feet and waving their hands in the air like they just don't care – have long been part of stadia entertainment, the term was only coined during the 1986 World Cup in Mexico City. Research into these waves (known also as *La Ola*) by Illés Farkas et al. [*Nature* 2002; 419:131–2] indicates that waves usually move in a clockwise direction at an average speed of 12m (*c.*20 seats) per second. They tend to be 6–12m (*c.*15 seats) wide, and can be instigated by only a few dozen spectators. Mexican waves at Lord's (the spiritual home of cricket) circle the ground but cease temporarily between the Allen and Warner Stands while the wave passes invisibly through the MCC Members' seats in the Pavilion. The restraint of the Members is usually accompanied by a humorous chorus of boos.

STAKHANOV & OBLOMOV

Alexey Grigorievich STAKHANOV (1906–77) was a Soviet coalminer famous in the 1930s for his hard work and efficiency. (Stakhanov's productivity was over 14 times the norm.) In an attempt to encourage such industrious output Stalin championed 'Stakhanovism' as a model for other Soviet workers. In 1978 Stakhanov's home town of Sergo was renamed in his honor.

Ilya Ilyitch OBLOMOV, created by writer Ivan Goncharov (1812–91), was a man so lazy that he did not rise from his bed for the first 150 pages of his eponymous novel. From this splendid character the notion of 'Oblomovism' developed – a state of languorous inertia, endemic in Russia's intelligentsia, caused by a fundamental idleness common in the Slavonic character.

SPORTING CATCHPHRASES OF NOTE

Sportscasters are bereft without a catchphrase. Here are some of the best:

Dick *'Oh my'* Enberg · Marv *'Yessssssss!'* Albert - Stuart *'Boo-yah'* Scott
Keith *'Whoa, Nelly!'* Jackson · John *'BOOM!'* Madden
Michael *'Let's get rrrrrready to rummmmmbbbble'* Buffer[†]
Phil *'Holy cow!'* Rizzuto · Harry *'Holy cow!'* Caray
Dick *'Yeah, baby!'* Vitale · Warner *'Let's go to the videotape!'* Wolf
Mel *'How 'bout that!'* Allen · Dave *'My, Oh, My'* Niehaus
Dan *'Simply en fuego'* Patrick · Verne *'Yes Sir!'* Lundquist
Chris *'He could…go…all.. the.. way!'* Berman[‡]
Jack *'That's a winner!'* Buck · Myron *'Okel dokel'* Cope
Darrell *'Boogity, Boogity, Boogity'* Waltripa

† Splendidly, Michael Buffer has managed to register his catchphrase as a trademark.
‡ ESPN announcer Chris 'Boomer' Berman (aka the 'Hunk-a Hunk-a Berman-Love') is (in)famous for coining nicknames for baseball players and other athletes. Here are some:

Roberto 'Remember the' Alomar	Chris Fuamatu 'Bad' Ma'afala
Bert 'Be Home' Bly even	Jason 'Look Ma, No' Hanson
Jim 'Two Silhouettes on' Deshaies	Chuck 'New Kids on the' Knoblauch
Andre 'Bad Moon' Rison	Sammy 'Say It Ain't' Sosa
Steve 'I've Got You Babe' Bono	Dave 'No Man Is an' Eiland

TISCHFUSSBALL &c

The game of Foosball is played around the world, on a variety of tables, with a variety of names: *Tischfussball* (German) · *Baby-Foot* (France) *Csocsó* (Hungary) · *Tafelvoetbal* (Holland) · *Bordfodbold* (Denmark) *Calcio Balilla* (Italy) · *Table Football* (Britain) · *Futbolín* (Spain) · &c.

———— DICKENS'S DISTINCTION OF IDLERS ————

Mr Thomas Idle and Mr Francis Goodchild … were both idle in the last degree. Between Francis and Thomas, however, there was this difference of character: Goodchild was laboriously idle, and would take upon himself any amount of pains and labour to assure himself that he was idle; in short had no better idea of idleness than that it was useless industry. Thomas Idle, on the other hand, was an idler of the unmixed Irish or Neapolitan type; a passive idler, a born-and-bred idler, a consistent idler, who practised what he would have preached if he had not been too idle to preach; a one entire and perfect chrysolite of idleness.

— *The Lazy Tour of Two Idle Apprentices*, 1857

———— THE UNLIKELY INVENTION OF CHESS————

John de Vigney, author of *The Moralisation of Chess*, asserted (somewhat bizarrely) that a philosopher called Xerxes invented the game of chess under the Babylonian King Evil-Merodach (*c.*?6BC) in the following way:

There are three reasons which induced the philosopher to introduce this new pastime: the first, to reclaim a wicked king; the second, to prevent idleness; and the third, practically to demonstrate the nature and necessity of nobleness.

———— FOCAL DYSTONIA, CHOKING, & THE YIPS————

The 'yips' are the involuntary and uncontrolled jerks, tremors, or freezing which affect certain individuals when they undertake finely controlled motor skills. In the world of sport, where fine movements can assume critical importance, the yips are most often associated with golf, especially putting or chipping, when a sudden jerk of the wrist can send a ball whizzing past the cup. According to Smith et al. [*Sports Med.* 2003; 33:13–31] yips-affected golfers add approximately 4·7 strokes to their scores over 18 holes. However, the yips can also affect a host of other sportsmen, including bowlers, snooker players, darts throwers, and even petanque chuckers. Considerable research has been undertaken into the yips, with some neurological evidence suggesting that they may be a form of focal dystonia. Such task-specific dystonias affect groups of muscles, usually when placed under repeated stress, and they include the commonly suffered 'writer's cramp'. The controversial suggestion that psychological factors like 'performance anxiety' or 'choking' might play a contributory part in such involuntary movements on the sports field is much disputed.

BUMBLEPUPPY

The term *bumblepuppy* has been ascribed to a variety of games: a form of racket-ball where the aim is to wrap a ball around a post to which it is attached with string (later popularized as swingball); a version of *al fresco* bagatelle played with lead balls; and most commonly, perhaps, any casual or unrefined game of bridge or whist. W. Somerset Maugham once wrote:

> Templeton isn't the sort of chap to play bumble-puppy bridge
> with a girl like that unless he's getting something out of it.

THE KNIGHT'S TOUR

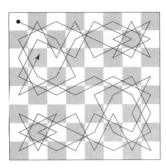

The Knight's Tour is a mathematical chess puzzle, the aim of which is to move a knight (as he moves in the game of chess) 64 times so that he rests once, and only once, on each square. A 'perfect' solution is where the knight finishes on a square one move away from his starting point, demonstrating that the tour could be continued *ad infinitum*. The route opposite by Monneron (*fl.*1776) is an example of a perfect Knight's Tour.

DOWN & OUT BOXING COUNTS

In Olympic boxing, if a contestant is knocked down, the referee begins a count of 10 seconds starting from 1 second after the boxer is considered down. (If the opposing fighter does not move to a neutral corner, then the referee will pause his count until he does so.) Once the referee has counted 10 and called 'out', the bout ends as a 'knock-out'. In any case, the round cannot resume until the referee has called 8, even if the downed fighter is ready to continue. If the same boxer goes down again, without having received a fresh blow, the referee continues his count from 8. If both boxers go down together, counting continues for as long as one is still down. A boxer is down if, as the result of a blow or series of blows:

> He touches the floor with any part of his body other than his feet
> He hangs helplessly on the ropes
> He is outside or partly outside the ropes
> He is in a semi-conscious state and cannot continue the bout

──────── SOME SPORTING SUPERSTITIONS ────────

TURFMEN

On the way to the races, if a turfman sees a name like that of the horse that is run that day, he takes it as an omen that the horse will win.

The initials of names on signboards or the headlines in the paper he is reading are all made to do service in spelling the name of the horse that is to be victorious.

To meet a funeral on the way to the track is a bad omen, although an empty hearse denotes good luck.

To dream of a horse that is entered for a race is lucky, but it will not win the first time it is run. It is sure to win the second time, however, and it is safe to bet on it then.

To meet a black cat brings bad luck, while a white cat is excellent.

To be followed by a strange dog is a good sign. To see a piebald horse means success.

To meet a cross-eyed man on the way to the track is very bad, but to meet a cross-eyed woman is lucky. However, a cross-eyed man of swarthy appearance foretells the best kind of luck.

To give alms to a blind beggar brings good luck, and to touch the hump of a hunchback man is a sure sign of success.

When the saddle girth of a horse gets loose, and the jockey is obliged to get off and tighten it, it is a sure bet that the horse will win.

Money that is won should be carried loose in the pocket, and not in a purse or wallet. It will then pave the way for more.

To find money on the track is a bad thing. It should be given away in charity.

BASEBALL PLAYERS

If any part of the player's uniform is missing, or torn, it means bad luck for the team.

If on the way to the game any name is encountered that suggests the name of one of the teams, that team will be successful.

Winning the first game often means that you will win the third.

Holding your bat in a certain way brings success.

When a team runs behind in its score a change of pitcher or catcher often retrieves their chances.

It is unlucky to play with a bat that is split, even if the damage is slight. A new bat must be procured.

It is a common belief that the team losing the first innings will win the game at the end.

——— SOME SPORTING SUPERSTITIONS cont. ———

A cross-eyed umpire is tabooed as a hoodoo†.

To have a 'southpaw', or left-handed pitcher, brings good luck to the team.

[† *The Oxford English Dictionary* gives its definition of a 'hoodoo' as one who practises voodoo, or a person or thing whose presence is supposed to bring bad luck.]

CARD PLAYERS

To play at the same table as a cross-eyed man is a sign that you will lose.

To lose your temper or get into a passion over the game is a sign of loss.

To have another person look over your shoulder while playing, or put his foot on the rung of your chair, is a forerunner of bad luck.

The four of clubs is an unlucky card to get. It is called the Devil's Bedstead.

To drop a card on the floor during a game is a bad sign, and means the loss of that game.

A green cover is the most fortunate to play on.

Most players have a lucky card which they touch with the index finger before sitting down to play. This ensures good fortune.

Singing while playing is a sign that your side will lose.

Playing with a fresh deck of cards is another way of forcing the goddess of fortune to be propitious.

Playing on certain days is unlucky for some, lucky for others. To play before 6pm on Fridays is unlucky.

Turning one's chair around three times is often resorted to to change one's luck.

It helps your luck to keep the chips carefully stacked up before you.

In Monte Carlo and other gambling places there is a belief that, after a suicide of an unlucky player, all those playing against the bank will win. When the news of a suicide becomes known, therefore, the card rooms at once fill with eager players.

To play cards on a table without a cover is considered unlucky.

If you wish a friend to win at cards, stick a pin in the lapel of his coat.

To lend money to an adversary with which to play is unlucky. To borrow money during a game is lucky.

Culled from
Signs, Omens, & Superstitions by
Astra Cielo (1919)

THE FOUR HORSEMAN OF NOTRE DAME

Notre Dame's 13–7 victory over Army on 18 October 1924, prompted Grantland Rice, a sportswriter for the *New York Herald Tribune*, to pen some of the most famous lines in sport's journalism. Rice boldly declared:

> *Outlined against a blue, gray October sky the Four Horsemen rode again. In dramatic lore they are known as Famine, Pestilence, Destruction and Death. These are only aliases. Their real names are: Stuhldreher, Miller, Crowley and Layden. They formed the crest of the South Bend cyclone before which another fighting Army team was swept over the precipice at the Polo Grounds this afternoon as 55,000 spectators peered down upon the bewildering panorama spread out upon the green plain below.*

SHOOTING NUMBERS

In shooting terminology two birds is a BRACE and three birds is a LEASH.

DUCKS AND DRAKES

'Ducks and Drakes' is the gentle art of skimming stones across the surface of a calm pond or river – the aim being to ricochet a stone across the water as many times as possible before it sinks. Smooth, flat stones and shells are the ideal ammunition for this sport, as the poet Butler notes:

> *What figured slates are best to make, On watery surface duck and drake*
> — SAMUEL BUTLER, *Hudibras*, ii 3

One of the first recorded uses of the phrase was by John Higins in 1583:

> *A kind of sport or play with an oister shell or stone throwne*
> *into the water, and making circles yer it sinke, etc.*
> *It is called a ducke and a drake, and a halfe-penie cake.*

It seems that ducks and drakes has long been associated with idleness and reckless squandering of money. This is not to say, however, that skimming stones does not have a serious side. The world record is currently held by Jerdone Coleman-McGhee of Wimbereley, Texas, for a toss that bounced 38 times across the surface of the Blanco River. And recent analysis by physicist Lydéric Bocquet (et al.) [*Nature* 2004; 427: 29] suggests that the optimal throwing angle between stone and water surface is 20°. Yet, J.B. Pick notes in his *Dictionary of Games* (1952) 'stones can dance on water with surprising gaity and verve but interest in the game soon lanuguishes'.

⸺ CLUE CHARACTERS, WEAPONS, & ROOMS ⸺

The tense board game *Clue* (called *Cluedo* in the UK) is initiated by the murder of Mr John Boddy (Dr Black in the UK) by one of the following:

Col. Mustard .. yellow	Rev. Green..... green	Miss Scarlett ...... red
Prof. Plum.... purple	Mrs Peacock ..... blue	Mrs White...... white

The murder weapons, and the rooms in which they are first located, are:

Dagger .... ballroom	Rope....... .... lounge
Lead piping .... conservatory	Candlestick .... dining room
Revolver .... study	Spanner.................... kitchen

Simpsons' Clue, set in Springfield, is premised on Chief Wiggum's investigation into the murder of wizened plutocrat Monty Burns. The suspects are: Homer, Marge, Lisa, Bart, Krusty the Clown, and Waylon Smithers. (Lisa Simpson, as Miss Scarlett, plays first.) The murder weapons are: the poisoned donut, the Extend-O-Glove, a necklace, a slingshot, a rod of plutonium, and a saxophone. The nine locations are: Barney's Bowl-A-Rama, Burns Manor, the Simpson house, Krustylu Studios, the nuclear power plant, the Frying Dutchman, Springfield Retirement Castle, the Android's Dungeon, & the Kwik-E-Mart.

⸺ SURF HEIGHT MEASUREMENT ⸺

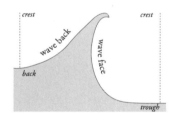

Traditionally, Hawaiian surfers used to measure the height of waves from the back to the crest. However, since the rest of the world employs the Wave Face as the standard measure, the 'Hawaiian Scale' (which tended to understate Face height by ⅓–½[†]) has fallen out of common usage.

wave face (ft)	description				
0–1	.......foot–ankle	4–5 .... waist–chest	7–10.. overhead & ½
2–3	.......knee–waist	5–6.......chest–head	10–15 .... double o/h
		6–7... head–overhead	15–20...... triple o/h

† Although there is some debate as to the origin of the Hawaiian wave measure, it seems to be part of an inverse machismo, whereby surfers underestimated the waves they rode.

⸺ THE HABIT OF SNOOKER ⸺

Playing snooker gives you firm hands and helps to build up character.
It is the ideal recreation for dedicated nuns.

— ARCHBISHOP LUIGI BARBARITO, *Apostolic Nuncio Emeritus*, 1989

——— MUHAMMAD ALI · PUGILISM & VERBALISM ———

Since his first fight in 1960, against Tunney Hunsaker, Ali has had 61 bouts: knock out 37; won 19; lost 4; knocked out 1. Below are Ali's most notable fights from when he became the heavyweight world champion:

date	opponent	where	result	round
25.02.64	Sonny Liston [USA]	Miami	W	TKO 7*
25.05.65	Sonny Liston [USA]	Lewiston	W	KO 1
22.11.65	Floyd Patterson [USA]	Las Vegas	W	KO 12
29.03.66	George Chuvalo [CAN]	Toronto	W	W 15
21.05.66	Henry Cooper [ENG]	London	W	KO 6
06.08.66	Brian London [ENG]	London	W	KO 3
10.09.66	Karl Mildenberger [GER]	Frankfurt	W	KO 12
14.11.66	Cleveland Williams [USA]	Houston	W	KO 3
06.02.67	Ernie Terrell [USA]	Houston	W	W 15
22.03.67	Zora Folley [USA]	New York	W	KO 7
28.04.67		*Suspended for refusing to go into US Army*		
08.03.71	Joe Frazier [USA]	New York	L	L 15
30.10.74	George Foremen [USA]	Zaire	W	KO 8†
24.03.75	Chuck Wepner [USA]	Cleveland	W	KO 15
16.05.75	Ron Lyle [USA]	Las Vegas	W	KO 11
30.06.75	Joe Bugner [ENG]	Kuala Lumpur	W	W 15
01.10.75	Joe Frazier [USA]	Phillipines	W	KO 14
20.02.76	Jean-Pierre Coopman [BEL]	Puerto Rico	W	KO 5
30.04.76	Jimmy Young [USA]	Maryland	W	W 15
24.05.76	Richard Dunn [ENG]	Munich	W	KO 5
28.09.76	Ken Norton [USA]	New York	W	W 15
16.05.77	Alfredo Evangelista [SPA]	Maryland	W	W 15
29.09.77	Earnie Shavers [USA]	New York	W	W 15
15.02.78	Leon Spinks [USA]	Las Vegas	L	L 15§
15.09.78	Leon Spinks [USA]	New Orleans	W	W 15‡
02.10.80	Larry Holmes [USA]	Las Vegas	L	KO'd 11

* won title · † regained title · § lost title · ‡ regained title

Key · KO Knock-out · W won by decision · L lost by decision

TKO Technical Knock-out · KO'd knocked out

ALI – THE TALE OF THE TAPE

Class .... heavyweight	Chest [expanded] . 45½"	Calf .... 17"
Height .... 6' 3"	Waist .... 34"	Ankle .... 10"
Weight 210½lbs	Biceps .... 15½"	Thigh .... 25½"
Reach .... 82"	Neck .... 17½"	Fist .... 12½"
Chest [normal] ..... 43"	Wrist .... 8"	Forearm .... 15"

Reach is measured from fingertip to fingertip as both arms are fully outstretched to each side.

—— MUHAMMAD ALI · PUGILISM & VERBALISM ——

This is the legend of Muhammad Ali,
The greatest fighter that ever will be.
He talks a great deal and brags, indeed,
Of a powerful punch and blinding speed.
Ali fights great, he's got speed and endurance;
If you sign to fight him, increase your insurance.
Ali's got a left, Ali's got a right;
If he hits you once, you're asleep for the night.

❦ [*On himself*] I am the greatest! ❦ I am not the greatest; I am the double greatest. Not only do I knock 'em out, I pick the round. ❦ I'm so mean I make medicine sick. ❦ [*On his boxing style*] Float like a butterfly, Sting like a bee. ❦ [*On pre-fight sex*] Only the nose knows, Where the nose goes, When the door close. ❦ [*On success*] You don't want no pie in the sky when you die; You want something here on the ground while you're still around. ❦ [*On Vietnam*] Keep asking me, no matter how long; On the war in Viet Nam, I sing this song; I ain't got no quarrel with the Viet Cong. ❦ Clean out my cell, And take my tail to jail. 'Cause better to be in jail fed, Than to be in Vietnam, dead ❦ [*Before Patterson fight*] I'll beat him so bad he'll need a shoehorn to put his hat on. ❦ [*On equality*] I know I got it made while the masses of black people are catchin' hell, but as long as they ain't free, I ain't free. ❦ [*On fighting*] There are no pleasures in a fight but some of my fights have been a pleasure to win. ❦ It's just a job. Grass grows, birds fly, waves pound the sand. I beat people up. ❦ [*To a flight attendant*] Superman don't need no seat belt. (*The reply was: 'Superman don't need no airplane, either'.*) ❦ [*On golf*] I'm the best. I just haven't played yet. ❦ [*On experience*] The man who views the world at 50 the same as he did at 20 has wasted 30 years of his life. ❦ [*On humility*] At home I am a nice guy: but I don't want the world to know. Humble people, I've found, don't get very far. ❦ When you are as great as I am it is hard to be humble. ❦ [*On Manila*] It will be a killer, and a chiller, and a thrilla, when I get the gorilla, in Manila. ❦ [*On speed*] I'm so fast that last night I cut the light off in my bedroom, hit the switch and was in the bed before the room was dark! ❦ When you come to the fight, don't block the halls, and don't block the door, For y'all may go home, after round four. ❦ King Liston will stay Until he meets Cassius Clay, Moore fell in four, Liston in eight. ❦ [*On Foreman*] I've seen George Foreman shadow boxing and the shadow won. ❦ This is a jet age. People are going to the moon and all. If you don't break a record, you're nothing. ❦ People come from all around, To see Cassius hit the ground. Some get mad; some lose their money, But Cassius is still as sweet as honey' ❦ [*On race*] In the US, everything is white. Jesus, Moses, and the Angels. ❦ Boxing is a lot of white men watching two black men beat each other up. ❦ [*On his lip*] Silence is golden when you can't think of a good answer. ❦

RUNNING THE MILE

The mile was originally a Roman unit of 1,000 paces (roughly 1,618 yds), but since then it has varied widely across countries and cultures. In 1592 the Statute Mile [Act 35 Eliz.I, c.6, s.8] was defined as 8 furlongs of 40 16-foot poles, or 1,760 yards – a definition which still stands. For many years it was assumed that a sub-four-minute mile was beyond the scope of human achievement. Yet as athletics grew in popularity during the C19th, and sophisticated watches were able to record minute fractions of time, so the hunger to break this theoretical barrier intensified. During the 1930s, 40s, and 50s, seconds were gradually chipped off the mile and, on the 6 May 1954, Roger Bannister managed to record the time of 3:59·4.

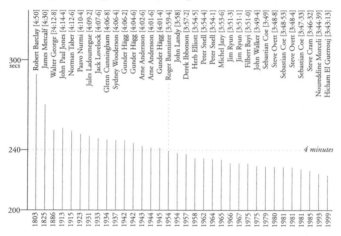

Although Bannister's record lasted only 46 days, it was clear as soon as his time was announced that the run had been something unique. As the London *Times* reported the following day: 'Bannister's performance … will earn for him athletic immortality no matter how soon someone else goes a fraction of a second better – or even a shade better than that.'

GOLFING HONOR

The 'honor' at a golf tee (i.e. the player who tees off first) is decided at the first hole by drawing lots. Thereafter, the player who scores the lowest on each hole has the honor at the next tee. If the scores are tied, then whoever had the honor at the previous hole tees off first at the next. During a game, the ball farthest from the hole is the first to be played.

GOALIE HOLES

Hockey's 5 'goalie holes' are the unprotected areas of net where the goal is vulnerable. In order of difficulty, they are: *stick-side low*; *glove-side low*; *stick-side high*; *glove-side high*; and the *five hole* between the goalie's legs.

PRO-RODEO EVENTS

ROUGHSTOCK EVENTS	TIMED EVENTS
bareback riding	*steer wrestling · team roping,*
saddle bronc riding	*tie-down roping*
bull riding	*barrel racing · steer roping*

THE LURE OF BASEBALL

'IN COURT' says the card on the *lawyer's* door,
'BACK IN TEN MINUTES' on many more;
'GONE TO HOSPITAL' or the *doctor's* slate
On another, 'SIT DOWN AND WAIT'.
'GONE TO THE BANK' on the *notary's* sign;
'ARBITRATION' that young *clerk* of mine
'BACK SOON' on the *broker's* book;
'COLLECTING RENTS' on my *agent's* hook.
They were all too busy, a matter quite new.
Very sorry was I, I had nothing to do.
Then I hied me hands to the baseball ground,
And *every man* on the grand-stand found.

— ANONYMOUS, *The Official Baseball Record*, 1886

MARCO POLO IN THE POOL

In the classic children's swimming game *Marco Polo*, a child is selected, often by means of a short race, to be the first Marco. Once all participants are in the pool Marco closes his or her eyes and calls out 'Marco', to which the others must reply 'Polo'. The aim is for Marco to 'tag' another child using these voices as a guide; once another is tagged, they must close their eyes and assume the mantle of Marco. A number of variants exist: if Marco suspects that a competitor has left the pool, they can shout *'fish out of water'* and if a child has left the pool they become Marco; alternatively, if Marco believes that someone has not answered 'Polo' they can challenge that competitor by name and, if they are right, the two swap identities.

CASTING HAND SHADOWS

Pig

Dove

Elephant

Greyhound

The shadows of things are greater than themselves; and the more exaggerated the shadow, the more unlike the substance.
— HERMAN MELVILLE

Rabbit

Goat

Camel

Puppy

POLO CHUKKAS

The game of polo is divided into *chukkas* of seven and a half minutes. At the end of each *chukka* a bell is rung, and the play is extended for thirty seconds unless the ball goes out of play, or the umpire calls a foul. [The last *chukka* of a match stops after seven minutes with no additional time added.] Between each *chukka* there is a three-minute interval – extended to five minutes at half-time. A full match lasts for six *chukkas*, but sometimes four or eight are played by mutual agreement. If, at the end of the final *chukka*, the scores are tied, then an interval of five minutes is called, the distance between the goals is widened from eight to sixteen yards, and additional *chukkas* are played until the deciding goal is scored. [The Oxford English Dictionary *gives the etymology of* chukka *as derived from the Hindustani* chakar *and the Sanskrit* cakra *meaning circle or wheel.*]

PILATES

German-born Joseph Hubertus Pilates (1880–1967) pioneered a system of exercises to develop and enhance strength, posture, and flexibility which he called CONTROLOGY. Pilates was a sickly child who from an early age studied anatomy to build up his body. He traveled to England in 1912 (apparently to work as a circus performer), but two years later, at the start of WWI, was interned as an enemy alien. While in the camps Pilates found work as a nurse and experimented with a range of techniques and makeshift equipment to rehabilitate the immobile. On his release, he used these skills to help train the German police force before emigrating to New York in 1925 and setting up a gym. Since then, the techniques of Pilates have been adopted across the world, and are used by a host of athletes, dancers, actors, sportsmen and women, as well as the infirm.

PRESIDENTS, GOLF, MULLIGANS, & BILLIGANS

Discovering the true handicap of any amateur golfer is problematic; with Presidential golfers the uncertainty is exacerbated. As with all players, their handicaps change over time, often improving when they leave office, and the security surrounding them aids the amateur's natural reticence. The table below, compiled from a variety of sources, is highly speculative:

Richard Nixon	12–14	J. F. Kennedy	7–10
Ronald Reagan	12–14	Bll Clinton†	12–18
George Bush	11–22	Dwight D Eisenhower	14–18
George W. Bush	14–15	Gerald Ford‡	12–17

† Clinton is perhaps the best-known exponent of the 'Mulligan' – a 'free' shot (often off the first tee) given and received among friends. Except, when the 42nd President uses them, they become 'Billigans'. It has been suggested that the 'Little Rock standard' is one tee-shot Mulligan and two fairway Mulligans per nine holes. In an interview with *Golf Digest*, Clinton claimed that his use of Mulligans was exaggerated, saying 'You'd be surprised at how many times you don't get a bit of good out [of them]'. However, he did admit, 'I let everyone have one off the first tee and then normally what I do when I'm playing with people is, I just play around and if somebody makes a terrible shot I say, "Well, take that one," and then I give everybody else one'. The word *Mulligan* has many meanings (a nickname for Irishmen; a train restaurant-car; a variety of stew; and a slang term for a cop) yet its link with golf is uncertain. The dubious Mulligan should be distinguished from the more noble 'gimme' – a put so close to the hole as to be 'given'.
‡ Ford once said: *The pat on the back, the arm around the shoulder, the praise for what was done right and the sympathetic nod for what wasn't are as much a part of golf as life itself.*

IDLE MONEY

Economists term uninvested funds or inactive bank deposits 'idle money'.

—SOME SPORTING, GAMING, & IDLING ON FILM—

❦ AMERICAN FOOTBALL · *Rudy*; *The Longest Yard*; *Knute Rockne* ['win one for the Gipper']; *North Dallas Forty* ❦ ARCHERY · *Deliverance* ['Goddamn, you play a mean banjo!'] ❦ AUTO RACING · *Grand Prix*; *Cannonball Run* ['God is our co-pilot!']; *Genevieve*; *Days of Thunder*; *Rebel Without a Cause* ❦ BASEBALL · *Bull Durham*; *The Natural*; *Bang the Drum Slowly*; *The Naked Gun*; *Pride of the Yankees*; *The Bad News Bears*; *Field of Dreams* ❦ BASKETBALL · *White Men Can't Jump* ['you either smoke or you get smoked']; *Hoop Dreams*; *Hoosiers* ❦ BOBSLED · *Cool Runnings*; *On Her Majesty's Secret Service* ❦ BOWLS · *Blackball* ❦ BOXING · *Raging Bull*; *Rocky* (see also p.143); *When We Were Kings* ['I'm so mean, I make medicine sick.']; *Ali* ❦ CARDS · *House of Games*; *The Cincinnati Kid* ['all you paid was the looking price. Lessons are extra']; *The Sting*; *Rounders*; *The Music of Chance* ❦ CHESS · *Casablanca*; *Blade Runner* (see p.119); *The Thomas Crown Affair*; *The Seventh Seal*†; *Harry Potter & the Philosopher's Stone* ❦ CYCLING · *Belleville Rendezvous*; *Breaking Away*; *American Flyers* ❦ CRICKET · *The Go-Between*; *Lagaan*; *Raffles*; *Wondrous Oblivion* ❦ FENCING · *Scaramouche*; *Hamlet*; *Die Another Day* ❦ FISHING · *A River Runs Through It*; *Jaws* ['You're gonna need a bigger boat']; *Big Fish*; *Grumpy Old Men* ❦ FOOTBALL (SOCCER) · *Fever Pitch*; *Bend It Like Beckham*; *Escape to Victory*; *Gregory's Girl* ❦ GOLF · *Tin Cup*; *Caddyshack* ['I won't be a caddy all my life. I'm going to carwash school in the fall']; *Goldfinger* (see pp. 64 & 120); *Happy Gilmore* ❦ HORSE RACING · *National Velvet*; *Bite the Bullet*; *Seabiscuit*; *The Killing* · ICE HOCKEY · *Slapshot*; *The Mighty Ducks*; *Miracle*; *Sudden Death* ❦ IDLING · *Ferris Bueller's Day Off* ['How could I possibly be expected to handle school on a day like this?']; *Withnail and I*; *Clerks*; *Barfly*; *Slackers*; *Waiting for Godot*; *Trainspotting*; *Smoke*; *High Fidelity*; *Mallrats*; *Swingers* ['You're so money, and you don't even know it!'] ❦ MARTIAL ARTS · *The Karate Kid* ['wax on, wax off!']; *Pink Panther* films ['Not now, Cato!']; *Enter the Dragon (&c.)* ❦ NIM · (see p.150) ❦ NOUGHTS & CROSSES · *War Games* ['Greetings, Professor Falken'] ❦ OLYMPICS · *Olympia*; *Walk, Don't Run* ❦ POOL · *The Hustler* ['This is my table, man. I own it']; *The Color of Money* ❦ RUGBY · *This Sporting Life*; *Up 'n' Under* ❦ RUNNING · *Chariots of Fire*; *Loneliness of the Long Distance Runner* ❦ SAILING · *Swallows & Amazons*; *Knife in the Water*; *Dead Calm*; *Pirates of the Caribbean*; *The African Queen* ❦ SHOOTING · *The Shooting Party*; *Gosford Park* ❦ SNOOKER · *Sleuth* ['whatever are you doing with that cue in your hand, dear boy?'] ❦ SKIING · *Downhill Racer*; *Hot Dog* ❦ SPORTS' AGENTS · *Jerry Maguire* ['Show me the money!'] ❦ SURFING · *The Endless Summer*; *Big Wednesday*; *Point Break*; *Blue Crush*; *Crystal Voyager* ❦ TABLE TENNIS · *Forrest Gump*; *Ping Pong* ❦ TENNIS · *Monsieur Hulot's Holiday*; *School for Scoundrels*; *Pat and Mike*; *The Royal Tenenbaums*; *Strangers on a Train* ❦ TENPIN BOWLING · *The Big Lebowski* ['You don't fool Jesus!']; *Kingpin*; *The Big Empty* ❦ TWISTER · *Bill & Ted's Bogus Journey*† ['Ted, don't fear the Reaper!'] ❦ † Both films feature games played against Death. ❦

———— KIPLING ON CHRISTMAS DAY SHOOTS ————

'Peace on Earth, Goodwill to men!' So greet we Christmas Day.
Oh Christian load your gun and then,
Oh Christian, out and slay!

— RUDYARD KIPLING, *An Almanac of Twelve Sports*, 1898

———— SOME MATCHSTICK PUZZLES OF NOTE ————

[a] remove 8 matches
to form 2 squares

[c] remove 9 matches
to leave no squares

[e] remove 6 matches
to leave 2 squares

[f] remove 5 matches
to leave 3 squares

[b] move 4 matches
to form 3 squares

[d] remove 3 matches
to form 3 squares

[g] move 3 matches
to leave 4 squares

[See p.160 for solutions.]

———————————— SIESTAS ————————————

One of the glories of idling is the *siesta* – a short nap in the middle of the
day popular in and around the Mediterranean but cherished equally in
countries across the world. The word derives from the Latin *sexta hora* –
literally the sixth hour which, in most temperate countries, is likely to be
the hottest. Perhaps because of dismal weather the English have tended to
eschew the practice of snoozing during the day as Noël Coward observed:

Mad dogs and Englishmen go out in the midday sun,
The Japanese don't care to, the Chinese wouldn't dare to
Hindus and Argentines sleep firmly from twelve to one
But Englishmen detest-a siesta.

—————————— BETTING ODDS SLANG ——————————

Evens	Levels, Scotch	7/1	Nevs
2/1	Bottle	8/1	T.H.
3/1	Carpet, Gimmel	9/1	Enin
4/1	Rouf	10/1	Cockle, Net
5/1	Hand	11/10	Tips
5/2	Face	33/1	Double Carpet
6/1	X's	100/30	Burlington Bertie

—————————————— YAWNING ——————————————

*[a] grotesque display of a mouth opening to its maximal width, in
association with a diaphragm contracting to an uncommon degree,
expanding the lung for an excessive intake of air, aided by a spasmodic
elevation of the pharynx blocking the customary gentle nasal airways*

— DR FRANCIS SCHILLER, *J Hist Neurosci* 2002; 11:393

Contrary to popular belief, it seems likely that yawning (also oscitation,
hiation, and pandiculation) has little to do with any need for extra oxygen
in the lungs. Not only do we breathe in far more oxygen than we use
(hence exhaled air contains oxygen), but ultrasound scans indicate that
fetuses yawn *in utero* even though their lungs are not ventilated. Research
by Steven Provine et al. [*Behav Neural Biol* 1987; 48:382–93] testing yawning in
environments with high levels of both CO_2 and O_2 indicated that
yawning 'does not serve a primary respiratory function and that yawning
and breathing are triggered by different internal states and are controlled
by separate mechanisms'. So, if we do not yawn because of so-called 'air
hunger', why do we yawn at all? Many theories have been posited: that
yawning raises brain power; that it serves to enhance our sense of smell;
that we yawn when our state of alertness changes; that we yawn when we
are plain bored; and so on. Indeed, if why we yawn is a mystery, so too is
yawning's contagiousness. The French proverb 'one yawn will breed
seven' is borne out by scientific studies as well as casual observation.
(Aristotle noted that 'like a donkey urinates when he sees or hears another
donkey do it, so also man yawns seeing someone else do it'.) It seems that
yawning can be contagious if we see it, hear it, think of it, or read about
it. Research, again by Provine, suggests that at least a quarter of those who
read this entry will yawn as a result. Recent investigations have explored
links between yawning and empathy, questioning whether yawning is
more of a social, paralinguistic act than it is a physiological necessity –
though nearly all of those who have written on the subject note how
utterly satisfying and pleasing it is to stretch out fully and yawn deeply.

CONKERS

Conkers are the inedible nuts of the horse chestnut tree – one of a group of trees (notably *Aesculus hippocastanum*) with five-lobed (palmate) leaves and conical clusters of flowers. (In America, the trees are called buckeyes.) As every school-boy knows, conkers are pierced with a skewer, and a length of string, twine, or shoelace, is threaded through the resulting hole. Players then alternate in striking at their opponent's conker, and the game ends either when one of the conkers is smashed, or when break-time is over. As might be expected from such an informal game, a number of variations exist. In some games each player takes three shots in a row. Another variant in play is that if the object conker is hit and spins in a complete 360° arc (known as the WINDMILL) the hitter is entitled to an additional shot. Depending on local rules, if the two conker laces become entwined during the game, then the first player to shout 'STRINGSIES' receives a free hit. Conker scoring is cumulative; a new conker is always a 'one-er' and its score increases by adding the score of its defeated opponents[.] For example, if a 'one-er' smashes another 'one-er' it becomes a 'two-er'. If a 'six-er' destroys a 'three-er' it becomes a 'nine-er'; and so on. Because of this unique historic scoring method, and because most conkers tend to be kept from one season to the next, scrupulous honesty in declaring the true score of a conker is a prerequisite of fair play. A host of (often underhand) techniques exists to temper conkers. These range from FREEZING or ROASTING, to soaking in VINEGAR or STORAGE in a warm dark place (the sock-drawer seems to be an ideal location). As a result of these rather dubious techniques most organized conker competitions insist that only 'house conkers' are played. Importantly, if either conker falls to the ground during a game, it may be stamped upon and crushed by an opponent unless 'NO STAMPSIES' is shouted.

† There is a school of thought which claims, somewhat vociferously, that new conkers should start as a 'none-ers'. This unsound and frankly reckless assertion risks making a mockery of the traditional scoring method. For if a conker's score is increased by adding to it the score of each defeated conker, a 'four-er' beating a virgin 'none-er' would remain a 'four-er' when, in fact, simple logic dictates that it should by rights become a 'five-er'.

FRENCH BOXING

La boxe française was a form of fighting, pioneered by Charles Lecour in the 1830s, where the use of the feet was both admitted and encouraged.

———— SOME SPORTING DEATHS OF NOTE————

Charles VIII of France, while walking in a tennis-court with his Queen, hit his head against a low door which caused his death.

Bradley Stone, Jimmy Murray, and Steve Watt are just a few of those who have died as a consequence of boxing injuries. A host of others, most famously Michael Watson and Gerald McClellan, have suffered serious disabilities.

Thomas Grice was killed when, during a game of football in 1897, he stumbled, fell, and punctured his stomach with his belt buckle.

In 1925 the jockey Frank Hayes suffered a heart attack during a race at Belmont Park, New York, and was in fact dead when he and his horse (Sweet Kiss) crossed the finishing line in first place.

Captain Matthew Webb, the first man to swim across the Channel (see also p.107), died in the insane attempt to swim the rapids and whirlpools below Niagara Falls. Of Webb's attempt, one writer opined 'his object was not suicide, but money and imperishable fame'.

Frederick Lewis, Prince of Wales, died having been struck on the bonce with a cricket-ball.

Louis VI died when his horse stumbled after a pig ran under it.

William III died after his horse stumbled over a mole-hill.

José Cándido became the first *matador* to be killed in the ring when he was gored to death by the bull 'Coriano' on 23 June 1771 at Puerto de Santa María.

In 1977 Bing Crosby died (albeit of heart failure) while playing a round of golf in Madrid.

After scoring the own-goal that gave the US victory over Colombia in a 1994 World Cup game, Andrés Escobar was gunned down outside a Medellín nightclub. It is said that the 27-year-old was shot six times by gunmen who taunted him by shouting 'Goal! Goal!'.

Rod Hull, the comedian behind (or inside) Emu, died at the age of 63 while watching the televised Champions' League quarter-final between Manchester United and Inter Milan in 1999. Annoyed by poor reception, Hull climbed onto the roof of his West Sussex cottage to adjust the aerial, but slipped and fell to his death.

Mal 'King Kong' Kirk (1936–87) died of a heart attack possibly precipitated by being crushed under the 26-stone girth of pro-wrestler Big Daddy.

Ivan IV 'the Terrible' (1530–84) died while playing chess.

It has been claimed that the Prime Minister Palmerston (1784–1865) died while having sex with a parlor-maid on his billiard table.

—— SOME SPORTING DEATHS OF NOTE cont. ——

During the 1982 World Fencing Championships in Rome, Soviet Vladimir Smirnov died when his opponent's foil snapped and pierced Smirnov's mask.

When Australia defeated England at the Oval in 1882, by 7 runs, the *Sporting Times* printed a mocking obituary to English cricket's death:

In Affectionate Remembrance of English Cricket, Which died at the Oval on 29th August, 1882. Deeeply lamented by a large circle of sorrowing friends and acquaintances. R.I.P. N.B. The body will be cremated and the ashes taken to Australia.

Some weeks later, an English team set off to tour Australia, beating them 2–1†. Afterwards a group of Melbourne ladies presented the English with the burnt remains of a bail which was entombed in a small brown urn about 4" high.
† *An Australian win was deemed unofficial.*

A Dutch woman was killed by a football-playing dolphin at a water park in Holland. The dolphin tossed a ball into the crowd as part of its act, but the ball struck the woman on the head, causing her to fall down a flight of stairs.

Presumably a number of sporting deaths were avoided after Italy won the World Cup in 1938. It is said that Mussolini sent the team a telegram before the match which read simply: 'Win or Die'.

Esteban Domeño became the first recorded fatality of the Pamplona Bull Run (see p.18) when he was gored to death in 1924.

In 1984, Jim Fixx, author of the *Complete Book of Running* and its sequel *Jim Fixx's Second Book of Running,* died of a heart attack while out jogging.

Apparently, all 11 members of the Republic of Congo football team *Bena Tshadi* died after being struck by lightning in 1998. Suspicions both of witchcraft and foul play arose when it emerged that the team they had been playing at the time, *Basangana,* all survived.

George Summers was the first man to be killed by a cricket ball while playing in a first-class game. While batting for Notts *vs* MCC in 1870 a delivery by J. Platts pitched off a pebble and struck his temple.

During the 1955 24-hour Le Mans, Pierre Levegh's Mercedes crashed into the crowd killing Levegh and over 80 spectators. As a mark of respect, Mercedes-Benz withdrew from all motor racing, only returning in 1987.

In February 2002, a bridge game held in Oslo to celebrate the 75th birthday of Willy Seljelid turned surreal when all four players were discovered shot dead. Police found a .22 hunting rifle at the scene, but were unable to ascertain which of the four men was the murderer.

—————————— YOGI-ISMS ——————————

Lawrence Peter 'Yogi' Berra was an astonishing catcher for the New York Yankees (1946–63), and was the American League's MVP in 1951, 1954, and 1955; he hit 358 home runs and appeared in fourteen World Series. Berra managed the Yankees and Mets (leading each team to the pennant) and was inducted into the National Baseball Hall of Fame in 1972. Yet, he is probably best remembered now for a wealth of pithy aphorisms:

You can see a lot just by observing.

Baseball is 90 percent mental and the other half is physical.

Listen up, because I've got nothing to say, and I'm only going to say it once.

We made too many wrong mistakes.

If you don't catch the ball, you catch the bus.

I didn't really say anything I said.

Just when you think you know baseball – you don't.

I think Little League is wonderful – it keeps kids out of the house.

If you can't imitate him, don't copy him.

Never answer an anonymous letter.

What difference does the uniform make? You don't hit with it.

I usually take a two hour nap from one to four.

It's *déja vu* all over again.

So I'm ugly. So what? I never saw anyone hit with his face.

[when asked the time] … you mean now?

If the world were perfect it wouldn't be.

… overwhelming underdogs …

If people don't come to the ballpark, who's going to stop them?

If you come to a fork in the road, take it.

A nickel ain't worth a dime anymore.

It gets late early out there.

The future ain't what it used to be.

——— FRENCH PLAYING-CARD CHARACTERS ———

One possible explanation of the identities of the 12 French court cards is:

Suit	King	Queen	Knave
Spades	David (Jewish)	Pallas (wisdom)	Ogier
Clubs	Alexander (Greek)	Judith (fortitude)	Lancelot
Diamonds	Caesar (Roman)	Rachael (piety)	Hector
Hearts	Charlemagne (Frankish)	Juno (royalty)	La Hire

─────────── ON JUGGLERS ───────────

The profession of the juggler, with that of the minstrel, had fallen so low in the public estimation at the close of the reign of Queen Elizabeth, performers were ranked, by the moral writers of the time, not only with 'ruffians, blasphemers, thieves, and vagabonds'; but also with 'Heretics, Jews, Pagans, and sorcerers'. In more modern times, by way of derision, the juggler was called a hocus-pocus, a term applicable to a pick-pocket or a common cheat.

— JOSEPH STRUTT, *Sports & Pastimes of the People of England*, 1801

─────────── SOME BOXING NICKNAMES ───────────

Jack *'The Lancashire Hero'* Carpenter · Ray *'Boom Boom'* Mancini
Bishop *'The Bold Smuggler'* Sharpe · *'Iron'* Mike Tyson
Alec *'The Chelsea Snob'* Reid · Tom *'The Bath Carpenter'* Gaynor
'Marvelous' Marvin Hagler[†] · Tommy *'The Hitman'* Hearns
Rocky *'The Italian Stallion'* Balboa · Jake *'Raging Bull'* LaMotta
Roberto *'Hands of Stone'* Duran · *'Smokin''* Joe Frazier
Apollo *'The Count of Monte Fisto'* Creed
Vinny *'The Pazmanian Devil'* Pazienza
Joe *'The Brown Bomber'* Louis · *'Prince'* Naseem Hamed
Oscar *'The Golden Boy'* de la Hoya
Tommy *'The Tonypandy Terror'* Farr
Larry *'The Easton Assassin'* Holmes · Donovan *'Razor'* Ruddock
Peter *'Young Rump Steak'* Crawley · James *'Bonecrusher'* Smith

† Marvin Hagler was the undisputed World Middleweight Champion from 1980–7, winning 13 of his 15 world title fights; and losing only to *'Sugar'* Ray Leonard. Marvin was so proud of his moniker that he actually had his name legally changed to Marvelous.

─────────── WOMEN & THE OLYMPIC MOVEMENT ───────────

Although the Olympic movement likes to present itself as inclusive and meritocratic, this was not always the case. The 'father' of the modern Olympics, Pierre de Coubertin [see also p.71], had opposed the inclusion of females at the Games, stating 'Olympics with women would be incorrect, unpractical, uninteresting and unaesthetic'. An early IOC statement on the question declared, 'We feel that the Olympic Games must be reserved for the solemn and periodic exaltation of male athleticism with internationalism as a base, loyalty as a means, arts for its setting, and female applause as its reward.' In 1900 the floodgates opened, and 11 women (against 1319 men) were permitted to compete at tennis and golf.

———————— STANLEY CUP WINNERS ————————

2004.... Tampa Bay Lightning	1964..... Toronto Maple Leafs	1925 .... Victoria Cougars
2003 .... New Jersey Devils	1963..... Toronto Maple Leafs	1924 ..... Montreal Canadiens
2002 ...... Detroit Red Wings	1962..... Toronto Maple Leafs	1923 .... Ottawa Senators
2001 ..... Colorado Avalanche	1961..... Chicago Blackhawks	1922......... Toronto St. Pats
2000 ...... New Jersey Devils	1960 ..... Montreal Canadiens	1921 .... Ottawa Senators
1999............. Dallas Stars	1959 ..... Montreal Canadiens	1920 .... Ottawa Senators
1998 ...... Detroit Red Wings	1958 ..... Montreal Canadiens	1919.............. *no decision*
1997 ...... Detroit Red Wings	1957 ..... Montreal Canadiens	1918 .... Toronto Arenas
1996 ..... Colorado Avalanche	1956 ..... Montreal Canadiens	1917 .... Seattle Metropolitans
1995 ...... New Jersey Devils	1955 ...... Detroit Red Wings	1916 ..... Montreal Canadiens
1994....... New York Rangers	1954 ...... Detroit Red Wings	1915... Vancouver Millionaires
1993 ..... Montreal Canadiens	1953 ..... Montreal Canadiens	1914....... Toronto Blueshirts
1992 ..... Pittsburgh Penguins	1952 ...... Detroit Red Wings	1913 .... Quebec Bulldogs
1991 ..... Pittsburgh Penguins	1951..... Toronto Maple Leafs	1912........ Quebec Bulldogs
1990........ Edmonton Oilers	1950 ...... Detroit Red Wings	1911 .... Ottawa Senators
1989.......... Calgary Flames	1949.... Toronto Maple Leafs	1910 .... Montreal Wanderers
1988 ...... Edmonton Oilers	1948.... Toronto Maple Leafs	Ottawa Senators
1987........ Edmonton Oilers	1947..... Toronto Maple Leafs	1909 .... Ottawa Senators
1986 ...... Montreal Canadiens	1946 ..... Montreal Canadiens	1908 .... Montreal Wanderers
1985........ Edmonton Oilers	1945..... Toronto Maple Leafs	1907 .... Montreal Wanderers
1984........ Edmonton Oilers	1944 ..... Montreal Canadiens	Kenora Thistles
1983 ...... New York Islanders	1943 ...... Detroit Red Wings	1906 .... Montreal Wanderers
1982...... New York Islanders	1942..... Toronto Maple Leafs	Ottawa Silver Seven
1981...... New York Islanders	1941 .... Boston Bruins	1905 ..... Ottawa Silver Seven
1980 ...... New York Islanders	1940....... New York Rangers	1904 ..... Ottawa Silver Seven
1979 ..... Montreal Canadiens	1939 .... Boston Bruins	1903 ..... Ottawa Silver Seven
1978 ..... Montreal Canadiens	1938.... Chicago Black Hawks	Montreal AAA
1977 ..... Montreal Canadiens	1937 ...... Detroit Red Wings	1902.......... Montreal AAA
1976 ..... Montreal Canadiens	1936 ...... Detroit Red Wings	Winnipeg Victorias
1975 ...... Philadelphia Flyers	1935 ...... Montreal Maroons	1901...... Winnipeg Victorias
1974 ...... Philadelphia Flyers	1934.... Chicago Black Hawks	1900..... Montreal Shamrocks
1973 ..... Montreal Canadiens	1933....... New York Rangers	1899..... Montreal Shamrocks
1972 .... Boston Bruins	1932..... Toronto Maple Leafs	Montreal Victorias
1971 ..... Montreal Canadiens	1931 ..... Montreal Canadiens	1898....... Montreal Victorias
1970 .... Boston Bruins	1930 ..... Montreal Canadiens	1897....... Montreal Victorias
1969 ..... Montreal Canadiens	1929 .... Boston Bruins	1896....... Montreal Victorias
1968 ..... Montreal Canadiens	1928....... New York Rangers	Winnipeg Victorias
1967..... Toronto Maple Leafs	1927 .... Ottawa Senators	1895....... Montreal Victorias
1966 ..... Montreal Canadiens	*(NHL take over Stanley Cup)*	1894.......... Montreal AAA
1965 ..... Montreal Canadiens	1926 ...... Montreal Maroons	1893.......... Montreal AAA

———————— ASCHAM ON ARCHERY ————————

Roger Ascham (1515–68), Cambridge fellow and tutor to Elizabeth I, is regarded as one of the fathers of toxophily (archery) because of his classic work: *Toxophilus, The schole of shootinge conteyned in two books* (1545). So important was this work that Henry VIII awarded him an annual pension of £10 and, when Ascham died, Elizabeth I is reported to have said 'rather would I have cast ten thousand pounds into the sea than have lost my Ascham'. Ascham's 'Five Partitions' of archery remain relevant today:

'STANDYNGE, NOCKYNG, DRAWYNG, HOLDYNG, LOWSYNG,
whereby cometh fayre shotynge.'

——— A GLOSSARY OF FOX HUNTING TERMS ———

All on...... what the whipper-in says when the hounds are accounted for
Babble........... a hound that *speaks* when there is no scent or no quarry
Biddable... an obedient hound
Blank .... failing to find a fox in a *covert*
Brush............................... .... the fox's tail
Burning.. .... a very strong scent
Burst... the first part of a run
Cap .... fee paid to have a day's hunting
Checking .... when hounds stop after a break in the scent or a disruption
Chop .... to kill a sleeping fox
Covert .... a wood, thicket, or copse used as refuge by the fox
Cut a voluntary .... to fall off one's horse while hunting
Doubling the horn..... notes very quickly blown to summon the hounds
Earth ....a fox's underground refuge
Fadge . ... a slow pace, somewhere between a walk and a trot
Gone to ground .... when a fox takes refuge in an *earth*
Holla.............. vocal call made to notify the huntsman of the quarry
Jink.. a sharp turn made by the quarry
Line .... the progress and direction of a hunt as it chases its quarry
Make a pack... count the hounds
Mask... ......the fox's head or face
MFH .... Master of Fox Hounds
Moving off .... leaving the meet to start a day's hunting
Music .... the sound made by the hounds when running
Mute.. a hound that does not *speak*
Rate[†]................................. .... to discipline or scold a hound
Riot[†]......... when hounds pursue the wrong quarry (deer, rabbits, etc.)
Scarlet[‡]........... .... the 'correct' name for a red coat
Sinking..................................... .... an exhausted fox
Speak .... when a hound barks as it hunts the *line*
Stern.. ....a hound's tail
Tantivy.. .... riding at full gallop
Unentered .... a young hound yet to hunt
View .... to sight a fox
Walking out................... .... daily exercise of hounds
Whelps .... puppies
Whipper-in ... a hunt employee who works as the MFH's right-hand man

[†] When hounds *riot* they are *rated* depending on the quarry they are chasing: Deer –
'ware haunch' · Hare or rabbits – 'ware hare' · Birds – 'ware wing' · Cars – 'ware motor'.
[‡] Many use the term 'pink' to describe hunting scarlet. This usage seems to derive not
from any color association, but rather from a (possibly fictitious) C19th tailor called Pink
(or Pinque) who apparently made the best hunting attire. However, since no records of
any famous tailor called Pink have been found, it seems likely that he never existed.

THE MODERN OLYMPICS

Season	Host city	Year	No. of sports	Male athletes	Female athletes	No. of nations	USA gold	USA silvers	USA bronzes	Most golds	No.
S	Athens	1896	9	241	0	14	11	7	2	United States	11
S	Paris	1900	18	975	22	24	19	14	14	France	26
S	St Louis	1904	17	645	6	12	77	81	78	United States	77
S	London	1908	22	1971	37	22	23	12	12	Great Britain	56
S	Stockholm	1912	14	2359	48	28	25	19	19	United States	25
S	Antwerp	1920	22	2561	65	29	41	27	27	United States	41
S	Paris	1924	17	2954	135	44	45	27	27	United States	45
W	Chamonix	1924	6	247	11	16	1	2	1	Norway	4
S	Amsterdam	1928	14	2606	277	46	22	18	16	United States	22
W	St Moritz	1928	4	438	26	25	2	2	2	Norway	6
S	Los Angeles	1932	14	1206	126	37	41	32	30	United States	41
W	Lake Placid	1932	4	231	21	17	6	4	2	United States	6
S	Berlin	1936	19	3632	331	49	24	20	12	Germany	33
W	Garmisch-Partenkirchen	1936	4	566	80	28	1	0	3	Norway	7
S	London	1948	17	3714	390	59	38	27	19	United States	38
W	St Moritz	1948	4	592	77	28	3	4	2	Norway	4
S	Helsinki	1952	17	4436	519	69	40	19	17	United States	40
W	Oslo	1952	4	585	109	30	4	6	1	Norway	7
S	Melbourne	1956	17	2938	376	72	32	25	17	USSR	37
W	Cortina d'Ampezzo	1956	4	687	134	32	2	3	2	USSR	7
S	Rome	1960	17	4727	611	83	34	21	16	USSR	43
W	Squaw Valley	1960	4	521	144	30	3	4	3	USSR	7

———————— THE MODERN OLYMPICS ————————

Season	Host city	Year	N° of sports	Male athletes	Female athletes	N° of nations	USA gold	USA silver	USA bronzes	Most gold	N°
S	Tokyo	1964	19	4473	678	93	36	26	28	United States	36
W	Innsbruck	1964	6	892	199	36	1	2	3	USSR	11
S	Mexico City	1968	20	4735	781	112	45	28	34	United States	45
W	Grenoble	1968	6	947	211	37	1	5	1	Norway	6
S	Munich	1972	23	6075	1059	121	33	31	30	USSR	50
W	Sapporo	1972	6	801	205	35	3	2	3	USSR	8
S	Montreal	1976	21	4824	1260	92	34	35	25	USSR	49
W	Innsbruck	1976	6	892	231	37	3	3	4	USSR	13
S	Moscow	1980	21	4064	1115	80	NA	NA	NA	USSR	80
W	Lake Placid	1980	6	840	232	37	6	4	2	USSR	10
S	Los Angeles	1984	23	5263	1566	140	83	61	30	United States	83
W	Sarajevo	1984	6	998	274	49	4	4	0	Germany	9
S	Seoul	1988	25	6197	2194	159	36	31	27	USSR	55
W	Calgary	1988	6	1122	301	57	2	1	3	USSR	11
S	Barcelona	1992	28	6652	2704	169	37	34	37	Former-USSR	45
W	Albertville	1992	7	1313	488	64	5	4	2	Germany	10
W	Lillehammer	1994	6	1215	522	67	6	5	2	Russia	11
S	Atlanta	1996	26	6806	3512	197	44	32	25	United States	44
W	Nagano	1998	7	1389	787	72	6	3	4	Germany	12
S	Sydney	2000	28	6582	4069	199	40	24	33	United States	40
W	Salt Lake City	2002	7	1513	886	77	10	13	11	Norway	13
S	Athens	2004	28	6548	4551	202	35	39	29	United States	35

--------- THATCHER ON THE IDLE YOUNG ---------

Young people ought not to be idle. It is very bad for them.

— MARGARET THATCHER, *The Times*, 1984

------- MONOPOLY: (UN)DESIRABLE PROPERTIES-------

The cheapest and costliest properties on a selection of Monopoly boards:

cheapest	*board*	*costliest*
Old Kent Road	London	Mayfair
Ronda De Valencia	Spain	Paseo Del Prado
Tire Yard	Simpsons	Burns Manor
Badstrasse	Germany	Schlossallee
Tupelo Boyhood Home	Elvis	Graceland
Boulevard De Belleville	France	Rue De La Paix
S.S. Swine Trek	Muppets	Kermit the Frog's Swamp
Dorpsstraat Ons Dorp	Holland	Kalverstraat Amsterdam
Yoda's Hut	Star Wars Classic	Imperial Palace
Chur Kornplatz	Switzerland	Zürich – Paradelplatz
Musgrave Road	South Africa	Eloff Street
Mediterranean Avenue	USA [standard]	Boardwalk
ΟΔΟΣ ΚΥΨΕΛΗΣ	Greece	ΛΕΩΦΟΡΟΣ ΑΜΑΛΙΑΣ
Palace Station	Las Vegas	The Strip
Auntie Em's Farm	Wizard of Oz	Home Sweet Home
South Street Seaport	New York (1994)	Trump Tower
Central Park	New York (1996)	The Plaza
Bronx	New York (1998)	Fifth Avenue
Västerlanggatan	Sweden	Norrmalmstorg
Biker Alley	Batman & Robin	Wayne Manor
Finsensvej	Denmark	Nytorv
Todd Street	Australia	Kings Avenue
Campo Grande	Portugal	Rossio
Crumlin	Ireland	Shrewsbury Road
Cheung Chau	Hong Kong (1997)	The Peak
Chep Lap Kok	Hong Kong (2000)	Victoria Peak
Gypsy's Covered Wagon	Scooby Doo	The Creeper's Bell Tower

--------------- RELAY RACE BATONS ---------------

The specifications of batons suitable for use in Olympic relay race events:
Length 28–30cm · Circumference 12–13cm · Weight >50gm

SLOT MACHINES

The US Nevada Gaming Commission defines slot machines as follows:

…any mechanical, electrical or other device, contrivance or machine which, upon insertion of a coin, currency, token or similar object therein, or upon payment of any consideration whatsoever is available to play or operate, the play or operation of which, whether by reason of the skill of the operator or application of the element of chance, or both, may deliver or entitle the person playing or operating the machine to receive cash, premiums, or merchandise, tokens or anything of value whatsoever, whether the payoff is made automatically from the machine or in any other manner whatsoever.

ON WOMEN RIDING SIDE-SADDLE

All women, of all ages and shapes, still look better side-saddle then ever they can astride. That's my opinion, and I stick to it. Granted, a girl with a lovely figure looks really ravishing in well made boots and breeches, astride a beautifully turned out blood-horse: but she would look even more ravishing were she to ride the same creature side-saddle, with a well-cut London habit and a silk hat.

— D.W.E BROCK MFH, *Introduction to Foxhunting*, ?1954

PLAYBOY vs THE OLYMPICS

Despite protests by Olympic authorities in Greece, the September 2004 edition of *Playboy* featured a host of female Olympians in revealing poses. Arny Freytag, *Playboy*'s senior contributing photographer asserted, 'this pictorial is different and fun and really shows natural and physical beauty … Lots of open spaces, blue skies, the chance to capture the athletes in motion – I know *Playboy* readers will like this'. The eight athletes were:

Amy Acuff............*high jump*	Haley Cope .....*100m backstroke*
Ineta Radevica . *triple & long jump*	Susan Tiedtke-Green ...*long jump*
Zhanna Block *100m*	Fanni Juhasz ....*pole vault*
Mary Sauer ....*pole vault*	Katie Vermeulen† *1500m*

† Katie Vermeulen is reported to have said: 'This thing is done to celebrate women and women at the Olympics, and it's not about boobs or butts … It's about strength and beauty and women who are strong and forceful, women who are posing to represent their strength and courage in their sport … So to me, it's much more than just posing for a magazine showing your body. It's not just an expression of what we do, but who we are.'

─────── WIGHTMAN'S TENNIS ABECEDARIAN ───────

Hazel Wightman (1886–1974) won numerous national and international titles in her long and distinguished career, earning herself the nickname 'the Queen Mother of Tennis'. In 1923 she presented the first Wightman Cup to the winners of the, now annual, US *vs* UK women's tennis match. In her classic 1933 book *Better Tennis*, Wightman presents her 'Letters of Advice' – an alphabet of admonitions for the aspiring tennis champion.

Always **B**e **C**oncentrate **D**on't **E**ver **F**air **G**et
Alert Better Constantly Dally Earnest Feeling Going

Hit **I**mitate **J**ust **K**eep **L**ess **M**ove **N**ever
Hard Instructor Jump Keen Loafing Meaningly New

Only **P**raise **Q**uash **R**elax **S**tand **T**ake **U**mpire
Over Partner Qualms Rightly Straight Time Usually

❧ **V**ary **W**ork **X**ceed **Y**ell **Z**ip ❧
Volleys Wiles Xpectations Yours Zip

───────── SPORT & THE SOCIAL DIVIDE ─────────

In the case of almost every sport one can think of, from tennis to billiards, golf to skittles, it was royalty or the aristocracy who originally developed, codified and popularised the sport, after which it was taken up by the lower classes.

— MARK ARCHER, *The Spectator*, 1996

───────── STROPS (BACKWARDS SPORTS) ─────────

There are a few sports where participants move predominantly backwards:

Swimming (backstroke) · High-jump (the Fosbury Flop†)
Tug o' war · Rowing · Abseiling (or rappelling)

A host of other sports exist where moving backwards plays a central part: fencing, ice-hockey, shot-put, gymnastics, diving, and curling (sweepers).

† The Fosbury Flop was invented by the American athlete Richard 'Dick' Douglas Fosbury (b.1947) as a revolutionary new approach to the high-jump. Fosbury rejected the traditional forward-facing 'straddle technique' and pioneered a method whereby jumpers arched backwards over the bar. After Fosbury won a gold medal at the 1968 Mexico Olympics his ungainly Flop was swiftly adopted as a standard approach to the high-jump.

THE CRESTA RUN

The Cresta is like a woman, but with this cynical difference:
to love her once is to love her always.
— LORD BRABAZON OF TARA

Situated in the charming village of St Moritz, in Switerland's Engadine Valley, the Cresta Run is a ¾-mile toboggan course which riders descend lying face-down on heavy metal 'skeletons' just inches from the ice. There are two starting positions: 'Top' for the experienced rider and, a little lower down, 'Junction' for the nervous. Speeds can easily reach 80mph and the accomplished rider will find himself 514ft closer to sea-level in under a minute. Little can be done in the way of steering, though riders attach metal rakes to their boots to help influence speed and direction. Since the run is carved anew each season from the Alpine snow, its exact structure and dimensions change from year to year – thus securing the Cresta Run's claim to be one of the last great amateur sports in the world.

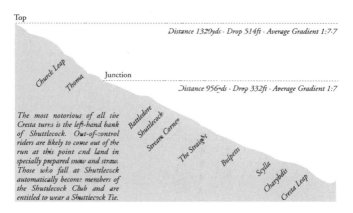

The Cresta is a powerful and attractive mistress.
She will stand no nonsense when you are learning the ropes, and many
and severe are the rebuffs that she administers to her most ardent suitors.
— SIR JAMES COATS

To date, only four riders have lost their lives on the Cresta Run but, as might be expected, minor and serious injuries are not uncommon. Before novice riders are permitted down the Run, all must attend the infamous 'death talk', at which the dangers of the Cresta are graphically illustrated by a life-size composite of just some of the X-rays riders have required.

STREAKING

The 1970s witnessed an explosion in streaking – an activity defined, rather splendidly, by *The Times* in 1973 as 'racing nude between two unpredictable points'. Although the relationship between human nakedness and sporting endeavour has links back to Greek times, sociologists trace the popularity of streaking amongst spectators to American college campuses which, at times, seemed almost over-run with students in the altogether. (In 1974 the Dean of Memphis State University became so exasperated by naked students he decreed that undergrads caught streaking would be 'suspended'.)

Although streaking has had its knockers, the activity is still popular and few sporting events are safe from the determined exhibitionist: Royal Ascot, Spain's Pamplona bull run, the Tour de France, international synchronized swimming, and even the world snooker championships have all been targeted. Perhaps the most infamous British streakers include Erica Roe (undisputed 'queen of streaking'); Michael O'Brien (pictured left); Michael Angelow; and Mark Roberts, who has more than 300 streaks under his non-existent belt, including Wimbledon, the Grand National, and even Crufts.

The campus streaking craze inspired Ray Stevens' novelty record *The Streak*, which was recorded in 1974, spent 3 weeks at No.1 in the USA, and sold over a million copies. In the same year, without doubt the most famous non-sporting streak was performed by 33-year-old Robert Opal, who sauntered naked behind David Niven at the Oscar ceremony. Opinion is divided as to whether or not the exposure of Janet Jackson's nipple by Justin Timberlake during Super Bowl 38's halftime show qualifies as even a very partial streak.

SPECIFIC CARD NICKNAMES

4♣........The devil's four-poster	**A♣** ...The horseshoe; puppy-foot
9♦..........The curse of Scotland	**4♣**..........The curse of Mexico
K♥..............The suicide King	**A♠** ....Old Frizzle
J♥ & **J♠**..........One-eyed Jacks	**K♦**........The man with the axe

The etymologies of these nicknames range from the obvious to the obscure. The 'suicide King', for example, is so called because the traditional French picture depicts him about to impale himself on his sword. A similar explanation is behind 'the man with the axe', and the 'one-eyed Jacks'. Considerable debate surrounds the naming of 'the Curse of Scotland', which has been linked to Queen Mary, the Battle of Culloden, the Massacre at Glencoe, Papists, and the design of the St Andrew's Cross. Francis Grose claimed in *The Antiquities of Scotland* (1789) that: 'diamonds ... imply royalty ... and every 9th king of Scotland has been observed for many ages to be a tyrant and a curse to the country'.

———————— MY OLD KENTUCKY HOME ————————

The theme now closely associated with the Kentucky Derby, *My Old Kentucky Home* was written in 1853 by Stephen Foster – the author of a host of classic American songs including *Oh! Susanna, Swanee River*, and *Camptown Races*. It seems that *My Old Kentucky Home* was first played at the 47th Derby in 1921 – and since 1936 it has been performed by the *University of Louisville Marching Band*, with only a few exceptions:

> The sun shines bright in the old Kentucky home,
> Tis summer, the people are gay;
> The corn-top's ripe and the meadow's in the bloom
> While the birds make music all the day.
>
> The young folks roll on the little cabin floor
> All merry, all happy and bright;
> By'n by hard times comes a knocking at the door
> Then my old Kentucky home, Good-night!
>
> Weep no more my lady Oh! Weep no more today!
> We will sing one song for my old Kentucky home
> For the old Kentucky home, far away.

———————— NEVADA'S FIGHTING FOULS ————————

Because of the local popularity of toughman, badman, ultimate fighting, and other varieties of mixed martial-art competitions, Nevada state law [NAC 467.7962] details a host of acts that constitute fouls in such contests:

Butting with the head · Eye gouging of any kind · Biting
Hair pulling · Fishhooking · Groin attacks of any kind
Putting a finger into any orifice or into any cut or laceration
Small joint manipulation · Striking to the spine or the back of the head
Striking downward using the point of the elbow
Throat strikes of any kind, including grabbing the trachea
Clawing, pinching, or twisting the flesh · Grabbing the clavicle
Kicking or kneeing the head of a grounded opponent
Stomping a grounded opponent · Kicking to the kidney with the heel
Spiking an opponent to the canvas on his head or neck
Throwing an opponent out of the ring or fenced area
Holding the shorts or gloves of an opponent · Spitting at an opponent
Using abusive language in the ring or fenced area
Timidity, including avoiding contact with an opponent, intentionally
or consistently dropping the mouthpiece, or faking an injury

EVEL KNIEVEL'S FRACTURES

Although the *Guinness Book of Records* records Evel Knievel as having broken more bones than any other man, it seems that they may have been taken in by Knievel's unrivaled skills of self-promotion. The 1972 edition of the book claims, for example, that in one year alone Knievel fractured 431 bones – an astonishing exaggeration which, through repetition, has simply added to the myth of the great showman. Below is a tentative schematic of some of the *major* injuries Knievel suffered during his career:

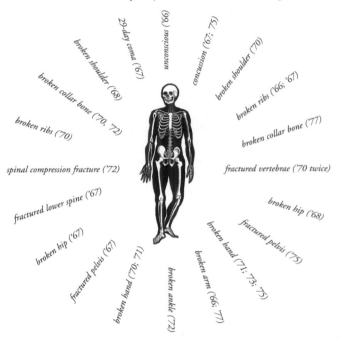

'Bones heal, pain is temporary, chicks dig scars, but glory is forever.'
— EVEL KNIEVEL [attributed]

SLEEPING & JERKING

HYPNOGOGIC JERKS
The spasmodic jerks which occur just at the point of falling asleep.

HYPNOPOMPIC JERKS
The spasmodic jerks which occur just at the point of waking up.

─────────── BOULE, BUTTOCKS, & FANNY ───────────

Boule tradition dictates that if a team fails to score a single point during a match they are expected to kneel and kiss the bare buttocks of the legendary voluptuary 'Fanny' *(rotondités de la plantureuse Fanny)*, whose image is to be found on pictures and sculptures in many a boule club.

─────────── SKI RUN DIFFICULTY · PISTE COLORS ───────────

Area	Easiest	Medium	Hard	Hardest
Europe	*(green[†])*	*blue*	*red*	*black*
North America	*green* ⊂ ...	*blue* □	*black* ◇ ...	*black* ◇◇
South America	*green*	*blue*	*red*	*black*
Japan	*green*	*green*	*red*	*black*
Australia, New Zealand	*green*	*blue*	*black*	*black*

† Green tends to be used in France. · [The grading of runs is often left to the discretion of individual resorts, and commercial pressures can influence how runs are graded. For example, there is a temptation to upgrade runs to black for reasons of prestige and, conversely, some runs that return skiers to their accommodation are downgraded to make them more acceptable to families. Runs marked with broken black, red, or broken yellow and black lines may signify 'itineraried runs', which are semi-official off-piste runs, usually of a difficult black grade, which tend to be patrolled, but not necessarily 'pisted'.]

─────────── SHUTTLECOCKS ───────────

Shuttlecocks have 16 feathers fixed into a cork base. These feathers[†] are taken from ducks or white geese and must be 64–70mm long; the tips of the feathers should form a circle with a diameter of 58–68mm; the base should be rounded at the bottom with a diameter of 25–28mm; the shuttlecock should weigh 4.74–5.50g. Shuttlecocks are classified thus:

Speed	weight	grain	for use
Slow........................	4.8g	75	at altitude
Medium slow	4.9g	76	in hot climates
Medium..........	5g	77................	at sea-level
Medium fast	5.1g	78.	in cold climates
Fast.......................	5.2g	79.............	below sea-level

Each classification adds approximately 30cm to the distance traveled[‡]. Grains are an alternative measure of weight used by manufacturers; 7,000 grains weigh approximately 1lb.

† Feathers from both wings are used, but the best shuttlecocks use feathers from only one side. Feathers from the left wing are said to be more stable in flight. ‡To test the flight of a shuttlecock, stand on the back line and hit it with a underhand stroke. A good shuttlecock will land not less that 530mm or more than 990mm short of the opposite back line.

—— THE QUEENSBERRY RULES OF BOXING · 1864——

1. To be a fair stand-up boxing match in a twenty-four foot ring or as near to that size as possible.

2. No wrestling or hugging allowed.

3. The rounds to be of 3 minutes' duration and 1 minute time between rounds.

4. If either man falls through weakness or otherwise, he must get up unassisted, 10 seconds to be allowed him to do so, the other man meanwhile to return to his corners, and when the fallen man is on his legs the round to be resumed and continued till the 3 minutes have expired. If one man fails to come to the scratch in the 10 seconds allowed, it shall be in the power of the referee to give his award in favour of the other man.

5. A man hanging on the ropes in a helpless state with his toes off the ground, shall be considered down.

6. No seconds or other person to be allowed in the ring during the rounds.

7. Should the contest be stopped by any unavoidable interference, the referee to name the time and place as soon as possible for finishing the contest, so that the match must be won or lost, unless the backers of the men agree to draw the stakes.

8. The gloves to be fair-sized boxing gloves of the best quality and new.

9. Should a glove burst, or come off, it must be replaced to the referee's satisfaction.

10. A man on his knees is considered down, and if struck is entitled to the stakes.

11. No shoes or boots with springs allowed.

12. The contest in all other respects to be governed by the Revised Rules of the London Prize Ring.

The Marquis of Queensberry was convinced (not unreasonably) that his son Lord Alfred Douglas ('Bosie') was having an affair with Oscar Wilde. On 18 February 1895 the Marquis left a card at the Albermarle Club in London which was addressed: 'To Oscar Wilde posing as a somdomite'. It was this misspelt card that prompted Wilde to bring his disastrous prosecution against Queensberry for libel and defamation. On Wednesday, 3 April 1895, the first day of the trial, Wilde testified to a verbal exchange he had with the Marquis: Queensberry · 'If I catch you and my son together in a public restaurant, I will thrash you.' Wilde · 'I do not know what the Queensberry Rules are, but the Oscar Wilde rule is to shoot at sight.' The trial collapsed, and after a second trial, Wilde was convicted of indecency, and sentenced to two years in prison with hard labor.

—— GOLDEN FERRETS ——

A GOLDEN FERRET is a golf stroke where the ball is holed from a bunker.

---------- THE NIKE 'SWOOSH' ----------

Alongside McDonald's 'golden arches', Coca-Cola's 'dynamic curve' bottle, the cross, and the crescent, the Nike 'swoosh' is one of the most widely recognized icons on the planet. The swoosh was designed in 1971 by the then graphic design student Carolyn Davidson, who invoiced just $35 for her work. The founder of Nike, Phil Knight, selected the design at the very last minute saying, 'I don't love it, but it will grow on me'. 12 years later, by which time the swoosh was known the world over, Davidson was given share options in Nike in recognition of her contribution to one of the most influential brands of all time.

Nike was the Greek winged goddess of victory, of which she is a personification. She was the daughter of the Titan Pallas by Styx (the river of the underworld), and sister of Zelos (rivalry), Kratos (strength), and Bia (force). During the battle between the gods and Titans she sided with the gods, for which she was rewarded by Zeus. Although Nike had few powers, she was considered lucky by the gods with whom she would ride into battle.

— PYRRHIC VICTORY, PHOCENSIAN DESPAIR, &c—

❧ A PYRRHIC VICTORY is one achieved at such a cost that it is almost indistinguishable from defeat. It seems the term derives from the bellicose antics of Pyrrhus (319–272BC), King of Epirus, who twice beat the Roman army but with casualties so crippling that one commentator wrote 'one more such victory and we are lost'. ❧ A CADMEAN VICTORY is one which immediately places the victor in a disadvantageous position. In Greek myth, Cadmus was the youngest son of Phoenician King Agenor. Cadmus slew a monster which guarded a fresh-water spring and sowed its teeth across the ground like corn. Immediately, an army of soldiers sprang up from the spot where the teeth had fallen and launched an attack. ❧ PHOCENSIAN DESPAIR describes a situation in which victory is snatched unexpectedly from the jaws of defeat. The phrase derives from the men of Phocis who, during Philip II of Macedon's reign (382–336BC), were subject to perpetual attacks from their neighbors for daring to farm the sacred field of Delphi. So great was the Phocensians' despair that they vowed to end their lives in a mass human sacrifice. However, just before mounting the pyre on which their women and children were stacked, the Phocensians mounted a last-ditch attack on their foes and defeated them. ❧ AMYCLAEAN SILENCE describes a reticence to speak that causes defeat. It derives from the inhabitants of Amyclae who were so exasperated by constant rumors of a Spartan attack that they passed a decree forbidding anyone to discuss the subject. When the Spartans actually invaded, the Amyclaens were too scared to mention it and the town was quickly taken. ❧

—NAISMITH'S ORIGINAL RULES OF BASKETBALL—

1. The ball may be thrown in any direction with one or both hands.

2. The ball may be batted in any direction with one or both hands (never with the fist).

3. A player cannot run with the ball. The player must throw it from the spot on which he catches it, allowance to be made for a man who catches the ball when running at a good speed if he tries to stop.

4. The ball must be held in or between the hands; the arms or body must not be used for holding it.

5. No shouldering, holding, pushing, tripping, or striking in any way the person of an opponent shall be allowed; the first infringement of this rule by any player shall count as a foul, the second shall disqualify him until the next goal is made, or, if there was evident intent to injure the person, for the whole of the game, no substitute allowed.

6. A foul is striking at the ball with the fist, violation of Rules 3, 4, and such as described in Rule 5.

7. If either side makes three consecutive fouls, it shall count a goal for the opponents (consecutive means without the opponents in the mean time making a foul).

8. A goal shall be made when the ball is thrown or batted from the grounds into the basket and stays there, providing those defending the goal do not touch or disturb the goal. If the ball rests on the edges, and the opponent moves the basket, it shall count as a goal.

9. When the ball goes out of bounds, it shall be thrown into the field of play by the person first touching it. In case of a dispute, the umpire shall throw it straight into the field. The thrower-in is allowed 5 seconds; if he holds it longer, it shall go to the opponent. If any side persists in delaying the game, the umpire shall call a foul on that side.

10. The umpire shall be judge of the men and shall note the fouls and notify the referee when three consecutive fouls have been made. He shall have power to disqualify men according to Rule 5.

11. The referee shall be judge of the ball and shall decide when the ball is in play, in bounds, to which side it belongs, and shall keep the time. He shall decide when a goal has been made, and keep account of the goals with any other duties that are usually performed by a referee.

12. The time shall be 2 15-min halves, with 5 minutes' rest between.

13. The side making the most goals in that time shall be declared the winner. In case of a draw, the game may, by agreement of the captains, be continued until another goal is made.

The Triangle, 15 January 1892

—————————— CITIUS · ALTIUS · FORTIUS ——————————

Below are Olympic results spanning the C20th. Although many factors must be taken into account (timing accuracy, equipment, &c.) they do suggest that we have indeed got swifter, higher, and stronger (see p.71).

Men's	1900	1920	1960	1980	1992	2000
100 meters	11·0s	10·8s	10·2s	10·2s	9·9s	9·8s
800 meters	2m01s	1m53s	1m46s	1m45s	1m43s	1m45s
Marathon	2h59m	2h32m	2h15m	2h11m	2h13m	2h10m
Long jump	7·185m	7·15m	8·12m	8·54m	8·67m	8·55m
Discus	36·04m	44·68m	59·18m	66·64m	65·12m	69·30m

Women's	1900	1920	1960	1980	1992	2000
100 meters	ⁿ⁄ₐ	ⁿ⁄ₐ	11·0s	11·0s	10·8s	10·7s
800 meters	ⁿ⁄ₐ	ⁿ⁄ₐ	2m4s	1m53s	1m55s	1m56s
Long jump	ⁿ⁄ₐ	ⁿ⁄ₐ	6·37m	7·06m	7·14m	6·99m
Discus	ⁿ⁄ₐ	ⁿ⁄ₐ	55·10m	69·96m	70·06m	68·40m

—————————— OLYMPIC DISCUS SPECIFICATIONS ——————————

♂ weight 2kg; diameter 219–21mm · ♀ weight 1kg; diameter 180–2mm

—————————————— SHEEP & SLEEP ——————————————

Counting sheep has long been employed as a method for encouraging somnolence and inducing sleep. The utter futility of the task (to non-shepherds) and the similarity of sheep to one another, weigh heavily on the eyelids. Although, that said, not all have found this method effective:

I couldn't get to sleep to save my soul. I counted ten million
sheep if I counted one — EUGENE O'NEILL, *Beyond Horizon*, 1920

One method is to count the sheep (picture them jumping over a low wall, one by one) using the traditional numbering system of English shepherds:

1 .... Yan	8 .... Overa	15 .... Bumfit
2 .... Tan	9 .... Covera	16 ..... Yan-a-Bumfit
3 .... Tether	10 .... Dicks	17 ..... Tan-a-Bumfit
4 .... Mether	11 ...... Yan-a-Dicks	18 .. Tether-a-Bumfit
5 .... Pit	12 .... Tan-a-Dicks	19 .. Mether-a-Bumfit
6 .... Tayter	13 .... Tether-a-Dicks	20 .... Jiggit
7 .... Layter	14 ... Mether-a-Dicks	(20 sheep are a 'score')

TOGS & DUVETS

A TOG is a unit of thermal resistance used to express the insulating properties of clothing and bedding. 1 TOG is the resistance that will maintain a temperature difference of 0·1°C with a flux of 1 watt per square meter or, put another way, the TOG value of a textile is equal to 10 times the temperature difference between its two faces when the flow of heat is equal to one watt per square meter. 1 TOG is roughly equal to the thermal resistance of a man's summer suit or a blanket of medium quality; 10 TOGs is the maximum it is practicable to wear. The TOG ratings of duvets vary by manufacturer but, as a rule of thumb, summer duvets are around 4·5–6·0 TOGs, whereas winter duvets have a rating of 12·0–13·5.

FISHING HOOK ANATOMY & SIZE

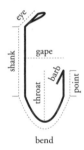

As a rule of thumb, the size of fishing hook needed is proportionate to the fish you hope to ensnare – although this is not always the case. Tench, for example, have mouths softer and smaller than one might expect from their size. A dizzying number of sizing systems have been advanced over the years (Redditch, Kendal, Carlisle, Pennell, to name but a few). However, because fishing hooks have so many variables of size, shape, and angle, a common system of sizing has remained elusive. In general, though, the smaller the hook number, the bigger the hook.

OPERATION

The medical board game *Operation* tests the dexterity of players as they perform a variety of surgical tasks on the sickly 'Cavity Sam'. Below is a list of the 12 operations along with the fees for doctors and specialists:

Doctor	Operation	Specialist
600†	*Brain freeze*	1200
500	*Bread basket*	1000
350	*Broken heart*	700
250	*Butterflies in stomach*	500
250	*Water on the knee*	500
300	*Wishbone*	600
200	*Charlie Horse*	400
200	*Funny bone*	400
150	*Writer's cramp*	300
150	*Adam's apple*	300
100	*Wrenched ankle*	200
100	*Spare ribs*	200
100	*Ankle bone to knee bone*	200

† To celebrate Cavity Sam's 39th birthday the makers of *Operation*, Hasbro, held a public vote to elect Sam a new ailment. Tennis Elbow received 19%; Growling Stomach, 27% but Brain Freeze won with 54%. *Operators* have to remove an ice-cream from Sam's head.

———————— THE ORIGINAL HAPPY FAMILIES ————————

family	*trade*				
Block.........barber	Bung.........brewer	Grits..........grocer
Bones.......butcher	Chip.......carpenter	Pots..........painter
Bun..........baker	Dip.............dyer	Soot ....sweep
	Dose. ... .doctor	Tape............tailor

All happy families resemble one another,
each unhappy family is unhappy in its own way.

— LEO TOLSTOY, *Anna Karenina*, 1875–7

———————————————— BUTTONS ————————————————

Buttons, like marbles, were a traditional tool of playground games,
though the 1859 handbook *Games and Sports for Young Boys* does warn
'we have heard some people say that games with buttons ought not to be
countenanced, as they induce boys to cut buttons off their clothes, and
transfer them to strings'. (Luckily, the authors dismiss this objection as
'silly and dishonest'.) It seems that children classified their buttons thus:

SINKEYS · metal buttons with a slight hollow in the center, with holes for the thread to be passed through. A plain SINKEY is a *one-er*; a SINKEY with letters around its edge is a *two-er*.

LIVERIES · heraldic or lettered buttons worn by livery servants. A small LIVERY counts as a *three-er*; a large LIVERY is a *four-er*, unless it bears a handsome crest, when it is a *six-er*. Bronze buttons, and those ornamented with fox's heads (etc.), are also *six-ers*.

SHANKEYS · buttons attached by means of a shank or loop of wire. The value of a SHANKEY depends on its size and beauty; if small and plain they are *one-ers*; if more ornamental they are *two-ers*.

Most games are played with *one-ers* – larger denominations are used as a means of exchanging capital. *Only metal buttons are played with.*

One classic button game is *Fitching at the Line*. A line about 2 foot long
is drawn on the ground and, from an agreed distance, the players 'pink'
for turns (i.e. the order of play is set by how close these buttons are to the
line). The first player then pitches two buttons at the line, aiming so they
rest as close to the line as possible without crossing it. The remaining
players follow suit. Once all have pitched, the player whose button is
nearest to the line claims all the buttons that landed over the line; the
remaining buttons he pitches into the air and those that land shank-side
uppermost he keeps. All the buttons that remain are divided up equally.

IRAQI PLAYING CARDS

One of the most curious packs of playing cards was issued in 2003 by the American Department of Defense. The pack of 'Personal Identity Playing Cards' featured the images of the fifty-two most wanted officials in Iraq:

♠A	Saddam Hussein	♦A	Abid Hamid Mahmud
♠K	Ali Hassan al-Majid	♦K	Aziz Salih
♠Q	Muhammad Hamza Zubaydi	♦Q	Muzahim S'ab Hasa
♠J	Ibrahim Ahmad Abd al-Sattar Muhammad	♦J	Tahir Jalil Habbush
♠10	Hamid Raja Shalah	♦10	Taha Yasin Ramadan
♠9	Rukan Razuki Abd al-Ghafar	♦9	Taha Muhyi al-Din Maruf
♠8	Tariq Aziz	♦8	Hikmat Mizban Ibrahim
♠7	Mahmud Dhiyab	♦7	Amir Hamudi Hasan
♠6	Amir Rashid Muhammad	♦6	Sabawi Ibrahim Hasan
♠5	Watban Ibrahim Hasan	♦5	Abd al-Baqi Abd al-Karim Abdallah
♠4	Muhammad Zimam Abd al-Razzaq	♦4	Yahya Abdallah
♠3	Sa'd Abdul-Majid al-Faisal	♦3	Mushin Khadr
♠2	Rashid Taan Kazim	♦2	Adil Abdallah Mahdi
♣A	Qusay Hussein	♥A	Uday Hussein
♣K	Izzat Ibrahim	♥K	Hani Abd al-Latif Tilfah
♣Q	Kamal Mustafa Abdallah	♥Q	Barzan Abd al-Ghafur Sulayman Majid
♣J	Sayf al-Din Fulayyih Hasan Taha	♥J	Rafi Abd al-Latif Tilfah
♣10	Latif Nusayyif Jasim	♥10	Abd al-Tawab Mullah Huwaysh
♣9	Jamal Mustafa Abdallah	♥9	Mizban Khadr Hadi
♣8	Walid Hamid Tawfiq	♥8	Sultan Hashim Ahmad
♣7	Ayad Futayyih Khalifa	♥7	Zuhayr Talib Abd al-Sattar
♣6	Husam Muhammad Amin	♥6	Muhammad Mahdi
♣5	Barzan Ibrahim Hasan	♥5	Huda Salih Mahdi Ammash
♣4	Samir Abd al-Aziz	♥4	Humam Abd al-Khaliq Abd
♣3	Sayf al-Din	♥3	Fadil Mahmud Gharib
♣2	Ugla Abid Saqr	♥2	Ghazi Hammud

The pack had 2 jokers, one lists Arab titles, the other Iraqi military ranks.

JAMES BOND ON GOLF & FEMALE BEAUTY

The difference between a good golf shot and a bad one is the same as the difference between a beautiful and a plain woman: a matter of millimetres.

— IAN FLEMING, *Goldfinger*, 1959

ON WINNING AND LOSING

KNUTE ROCKNE · *Norwegian-born American football coach* · Show me a good and gracious loser, and I'll show you a failure.

IAN FLEMING · The gain to the winner is, in some odd way, always less than the loss to the loser.

TOMMY HITCHCOCK · *US polo player and aviator* · Lose as if you like it; win as if you were used to it.

HENRY 'RED' SANDERS · *American football coach* · Sure, winning isn't everything. It's the only thing.

ERNEST HEMINGWAY · You make your own luck ... You know what makes a good loser? Practice.

VINCE LOMBARDI · Show me a good loser and I'll show you a loser.

MACBETH: If we should fail?
LADY MACBETH: We fail!
But screw your courage to the sticking place, And we'll not fail. [*Macbeth*, I.vii.]

ANONYMOUS · Quitters never win. Winners never quit.

RICHARD NIXON · *writing to Senator Edward Kennedy after the Chappaquiddick debacle in 1969* · A man's not finished when he's defeated; he's finished when he quits.

MARIO PUZO · Show me a gambler and I'll show you a loser; show me a hero and I'll show you a corpse.

CHRIS EVERT · In tennis, at the end of the day you're a winner or a loser. You know exactly where you stand ... I don't need that anymore. I don't need my happiness, my well-being, to be based on winning and losing.

GALEAZZO CIANO · Victory has a hundred fathers but defeat is an orphan. *(This phrase was quoted by President John F. Kennedy after the 1961 Bay of Pigs disaster.)*

MARTINA NAVRATILOVA · The moment of victory is much too short to live for that and nothing else.

MAX BEERBOHM · There is much to be said for failure. It is more interesting than success.

PETER MANDELSON · I am a fighter, not a quitter.

LOUIS KRONENBERGER · The technique of winning is so shoddy, the terms of winning are so ignoble, the tenure of winning is so brief; and the specter of the has-been – a shameful rather than a pitiable sight these days – brings a sudden chill even to our sunlit moments.

SENECA · Success is not greedy, as people think, but insignificant. That's why it satisfies nobody.

JEAN-PAUL SARTRE · If a victory is told in detail, one can no longer distinguish it from a defeat.

———————— ROLLER-SKATES & MIRRORS————————

It is claimed that the Belgian Joseph Merlin first invented roller-skates in 1760. Apparently, Merlin wore his skates to a masquerade ball held at Carlisle House in Soho Square, London – but was so unstable on them that he destroyed a mirror worth over £500, and badly wounded himself.

———————————— ELEPHANT POLO ————————————

It should come as no surprise that a sport as idiosyncratic as elephant polo should have been dreamt up in a St Moritz bar by two dedicated riders of the Cresta Run (see p.53). The brainchild of Jim Edwards, and Olympic tobogganer James Manclark, elephant polo is governed by the World Elephant Polo Association (WEPA), which hosts its annual tournaments on a grass airstrip just outside the Royal Chitwan National Park, in Nepal. Although many similarities exist between elephant polo and its equestrian forerunner, a number of modifications have been made to allow for the inherent differences between horses and pachyderms:

The elephant polo pitch is 120m × 70m (¾ that of a traditional pitch), with 4 players on each side.

Although the game used to be played with footballs, the elephants quickly developed a passion for stamping on the balls until they exploded. Nowadays standard polo balls are used.

Each elephant has two people on its back: the player who strikes the ball, and the *mahout* who handles and steers the elephant.

A game is comprised of two 10-minute chukkas, with a 15-minute interval during which elephants and ends are changed.

To avoid instinctive but dangerous herding behavior, no team may have more than 3 elephants in one half at any time.

A foul is committed if an elephant lies down in front of the goal-mouth. Similarly, a foul is committed if an elephant picks up the ball with its trunk.

Sticks range from 6–9ft in length, varying on the size of the elephant, and have a traditional mallet head.

Smaller, more nimble elephants are favored for offensive roles, though older female elephants are often placed defensively near goal to intimidate male competition.

To ensure that the elephants do not overheat, games are not played after midday.

'Ball-boys' are responsible for removing piles of dung, to avoid the possibility of balls becoming ensnared, or excrement being flung by swinging mallets.

CONTRACT BRIDGE SCORING

TRUMPS				*for each trick over 6 bid & made*	NO TRUMPS	
♣	♦	♠	♥		1st trick	Others
20	20	30	30	Undoubled	40	30
40	40	60	60	Doubled	80	60
80	80	120	120	Redoubled	160	120

The 1st to score 100 points below the line, in 1 or more hands, wins a game

HONORS

Scored above the line by either side

Any 4 AKQJT in a suit bid 100
All 5 AKQJT in a suit bid 150
All 4 Aces in No Trump bid .. 150

RUBBER BONUS

Two-game rubber 700
Three-game rubber 500
Unfinished rubber – 1 game .. 300
Part Score 100

PREMIUMS – *scored above the line for the Declarer*

Making Doubled contract ..... 50 | Making Redoubled contract .. 100

NOT VULNERABLE	*over tricks*	VULNERABLE
Trick value .... Uncoubled .. .. Trick value
100 .... Doubled 200
200 .... Redoubled 400
500 .... Small Slam bonus (bid of 6) 750
1000 .... Grand Slam bonus (bid of 7) 1500

NOT VULNERABLE		*failed contract penalty*		VULNERABLE		
Undoubled	Doubled	Redoubled	Undertricks	Undoubled	Doubled	Redoubled
50	100	200	one	100	200	400
100	300	600	two	200	500	1000
150	500	1000	three	300	800	1600
200	800	1600	four	400	1100	2200
250	1100	2200	five	500	1400	2800
300	1400	2800	six	600	1700	3400

SPHAIRISTIKE

Sphairistike is the name by which lawn tennis used to be known. The game was invented by Major Walter Clopton Wingfield, who introduced it in 1873 to a Christmas party in Nantclywd, Wales. The game borrowed heavily from the existing games of Royal Tennis and badminton and was played on an hourglass-shaped court with a net 5' high. The Major named the game *Sphairistike* (Greek for 'ball playing') but affectionately called it *Sticky*. As the game's popularity grew this unpronounceable name was rejected in favor of something less silly, and 'lawn tennis' was born.

No.	Date	Winner	Loser	MVP	'Theme'	National Anthem performed by
I	15-01-67	GREEN BAY 35	Kansas City 10	Bart Starr	—	Unis of Arizona & Michigan Bands
II	14-01-68	GREEN BAY 33	Oakland 14	Bart Starr	—	Grambling University Band
III	12-01-69	NY JETS 16	Baltimore 7	Joe Namath	America Thanks	Anita Bryant
IV	11-01-70	KANSAS CITY 23	Minnesota 7	Len Dawson	Mardi Gras	Al Hirt
V	17-01-71	BALTIMORE 16	Dallas 13	Chuck Howley	—	Tommy Loy (trumpeter)
VI	16-01-72	DALLAS 24	Miami 3	Roger Staubach	Salute to Louis Armstrong	US Airforce Academy Chorale
VII	14-01-73	MIAMI 14	Washington 7	Jake Scott	Happiness Is	Holy Angels Church
VIII	13-01-74	MIAMI 24	Minnesota 7	Larry Csonka	A Musical America	Charlie Pride
IX	12-01-75	PITTSBURGH 16	Minnesota 6	Franco Harris	Tribute to Duke Ellington	Grambling University Band
X	18-01-76	PITTSBURGH 21	Dallas 17	Lynn Swann	Bicentennial Tribute	Tom Sullivan
XI	09-01-77	OAKLAND 32	Minnesota 14	Fred Biletnikoff	It's a Small World	Vicki Carr
XII	15-01-78	DALLAS 27	Denver 10	White & Martin	From Paris to Paris of America	Phyllis Kelly
XIII	21-01-79	PITTSBURGH 35	Dallas 31	Terry Bradshaw	Carnival Salute to Caribbean	The Colgate Thirteen
XIV	20-01-80	PITTSBURGH 31	LA Rams 19	Terry Bradshaw	Salute to the Big Band Era	Cheryl Ladd
XV	25-01-81	OAKLAND 27	Philadelphia 10	Jim Plunkett	Mardi Gras Festival	Helen O'Connell
XVI	24-01-82	SAN FRANCISCO 26	Cincinnati 21	Joe Montana	Salute to the '60s and Motown	Diana Ross
XVII	30-01-83	WASHINGTON 27	Miami 17	John Riggins	KaleidoSUPERscope	Leslie Esterbrook
XVIII	22-01-84	LA RAIDERS 38	Washington 9	Marcus Allen	Superstars of the Silver Screen	Barry Manilow
XIX	20-01-85	SAN FRANCISCO 38	Miami 16	Joe Montana	World of Children's Dreams	Children's Choir of SF
XX	26-01-86	CHICAGO 46	New England 10	Richard Dent	Beat of the Future	Wynton Marsalis
XXI	25-01-87	NY GIANTS 39	Denver 20	Phil Simms	Hollywood's 100th Anniversary	Neil Diamond
XXII	31-01-88	WASHINGTON 42	Denver 10	Doug Williams	Something Grand	Herb Alpert
XXIII	22-01-89	SAN FRANCISCO 20	Cincinnati 16	Jerry Rice	Be Bop Bamboozled	Billy Joel
XXIV	28-01-90	SAN FRANCISCO 55	Denver 10	Joe Montana	New Orleans / Snoopy's 40th Birthday	Aaron Neville

No.	Date	Winner	Loser	MVP	'Theme'	National Anthem performed by
XXV	27-01-91	NY GIANTS 20	Buffalo 19	Ottis Anderson	25 Years of Super Bowl	Whitney Houston
XXVI	26-01-92	WASHINGTON 37	Buffalo 24	Mark Rypien	Winter Magic	Harry Connick Jr
XXVII	31-01-93	DALLAS 52	Buffalo 17	Troy Aikman	Heal the World	Garth Brooks
XXVIII	30-01-94	DALLAS 30	Buffalo 13	Emmit Smith	Rockin' Country Sunday	Natalie Cole
XXIX	29-01-95	SAN FRANCISCO 49	San Diego 26	Steve Young	Indiana Jones	Kathie Lee Gifford
XXX	28-01-96	DALLAS 27	Pittsburgh 17	Larry Brown	30 Years of Super Bowl	Vanessa Williams
XXXI	26-01-97	GREEN BAY 35	New England 21	Desmond Howard	Blues Brothers Bash	Luther Vandross
XXXII	25-01-98	DENVER 31	Green Bay 24	Terrell Davis	Motown's 40th Anniversary	Jewel
XXXIII	31-01-99	DENVER 34	Atlanta 19	John Elway	Soul, Salsa and Swing	Cher
XXXIV	30-01-00	ST LOUIS 23	Tennessee 16	Kurt Warner	Tapestry of Nations	Faith Hill
XXXV	28-01-01	BALTIMORE 34	NY Giants 7	Ray Lewis	—	Backstreet Boys
XXXVI	03-02-02	NEW ENGLAND 20	St Louis 17	Tom Brady	—	Mariah Carey
XXXVII	26-01-03	TAMPA BAY 48	Oakland 21	Dexter Jackson	—	Dixie Chicks
XXXVIII	01-02-04	NEW ENGLAND 32	Carolina 29	Tom Brady	—	Beyonce Knowles
XXXIX	06-02-05	NEW ENGLAND 24	Philadelphia 21	Deion Branch	—	combined Academy choir of US Armed Forces

A few notable Super Bowl TV commercials:

'72	*Noxema* 'cream your face'	'89	*AmEx* Dana Carvey & Jon Lovitz
'74	*Master Lock* 'Marksman' padlocks	'93	*McDonald's* 'Showdown' of horse
'77	*Xerox* 'Monks' copying manuscript	'95	*Budweiser* 'Frogs' ribbeting
'79	*Coke* 'Mean Joe Green'	'96	*Budweiser* 'Clydesdales Play Ball' in snow
'84	*Apple* '1984' with sledgehammer	'97	*Pepsi* 'Dancing Bears' & YMCA
'87	*Pepsi* 'Apartment 10G' & Michael J. Fox	'95	*Pepsi* 'Diner' with truck driver
		'95	*Pepsi* 'Sucked In' boy & his bottle
		'99	*Budweiser* 'Dalmatians' reunited
		'00	*Electronic Data Systems* 'Herding Cats'
		'00	*Budweiser* 'Rex's Bad Day' dog & van
		'01	*Budweiser* 'Cedric' hot date & bottle
		'02	*Levi's* 'crazy-legs' / Giuliani's NY tribute
		'03	*FedEx* castaway package
		'04	*Budweiser* Donkey / *Pepsi* Hendrix
		'05	*Emerald Nuts* 'disappearing unicorn'
		'05	*GoDaddy* Super Bowl censorship

MARTIAL ART MEANINGS

Martial art	*translation*
AIDO	attacking from the scabbard
AIKIDO	the way of harmony
BAGUAZHANG	eight shapes palms
BUDO	the warrior path
BUGEI	the warrior arts
HAPKIDO	way of coordinated power
JEET KUNE DO	way of the intercepting fist
JUDO	the gentle way
JUJITSU	the gentle technique
KARATE	the way of the empty hand
KENDO	the way of the sword
KENPO	way of the fist
KUNG FU	one who is highly skilled
NINJUTSU	art of invisibility
TAE KWAN DO	way of the hands and feet
TAI CHI	great supreme absolute

SYNCHRONIZED SWIMMING: DOLPHOLINA

Dolpholina is just one of FINA's elegant synchronized swimming moves:

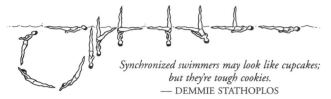

Synchronized swimmers may look like cupcakes; but they're tough cookies.
— DEMMIE STATHOPLOS

THE SHILL AND THE PROP

In US casino terminology a SHILL is a player (paid an hourly wage by the House) who uses the House's money to drum up business by playing at slow tables. Any money made by the SHILL is returned to the House. In contrast, PROPOSITION PLAYERS, or PROPS, play with their own money (while receiving a small wage), keeping any profits but shouldering their losses. Both SHILLS and PROPS work under the direction of the House staff, who will move them as required from game to game. In many casinos strict rules exist governing how SHILLS and PROPS may play each game, and requiring the House to identify the paid players if so requested.

THE OLYMPIC CREED, MOTTO, & OATHS

Although usually attributed to Pierre de Coubertin (1863–1937), the first President of the International Olympic Committee, it seems that the Olympic creed was inspired by a sermon given in St Paul's Cathedral by Ethelbert Talbot, the Bishop of Central Pennsylvania, on 19 July 1908.

The most important thing in the Olympic Games is not to win but to take part, just as the most important thing in life is not the triumph but the struggle. The essential thing is not to have conquered but to have fought well.

De Coubertin is also responsible for instituting the Olympic motto:

CITIUS · ALTIUS · FORTIUS   *swifter · higher · stronger*   (see p.61)

This time de Coubertin borrowed from the French Dominican preacher Father Henri Didon (1840–1900), over whose door the motto was carved. The Olympic Oath, instituted in 1920 and updated in 2000 to address the issue of doping, is taken on behalf of all athletes by a member of the host team. Holding a corner of their national flag, the athlete declaims from the rostrum, in front of the assembled flag-bearers of other nations:

In the name of all the competitors, I promise that we shall take part in these Olympic Games, respecting and abiding by the rules which govern them, committing ourselves to a sport without doping and without drugs, in the true spirit of sportsmanship, for the glory of sport and the honor of our teams.

Since 1972, an officials' oath has also been read by a host-country official:

In the name of all the judges and officials, I promise that we shall officiate in these Olympic Games with complete impartiality, respecting and abiding by the rules which govern them, in the true spirit of sportsmanship.

WIMBLEDON RAIN-WARNING CODES

A numerical system is employed at Wimbledon to alert and instruct those in charge of covering courts when rain or inclement weather is expected:

1	be on standby, by the court, as there is a concern that it may rain
2	cover the court
3	inflate covers
4	deflate covers (when rain has stopped)
5	uncover court
6	dress the courts for play

— SCRABBLE LETTERS AROUND THE WORLD —

Tile	Turkish		French		German		English		Spanish	
	value	*no*	*value*	*no*	*value*	*no*	*value*	*no*	*value*	*no*
A	1	12	1	9	1	5	1	9	1	11
Ä	N/A	N/A	N/A	N/A	6	1	N/A	N/A	N/A	N/A
B	3	2	3	2	3	2	3	2	3	3
C	4	2	3	2	4	2	3	2	2	4
Ç	4	2	N/A	N/A	N/A	N/A	N/A	N/A	N/A	N/A
D	3	2	2	3	1	4	2	4	2	4
E	1	8	1	15	1	15	1	12	1	11
F	7	1	4	2	4	2	4	2	4	2
G	5	1	2	2	2	3	2	3	2	2
Ğ	8	1	N/A	N/A	N/A	N/A	N/A	N/A	N/A	N/A
H	5	1	4	2	2	4	4	2	4	2
I	2	4	1	8	1	6	1	9	1	6
İ	1	7	N/A	N/A	N/A	N/A	N/A	N/A	N/A	N/A
J	10	1	8	1	6	1	8	1	6	2
K	1	7	10	1	4	2	5	1	8	1
L	1	7	1	5	2	3	1	4	1	4
LL	N/A	N/A	N/A	N/A	N/A	N/A	N/A	N/A	8	1
M	2	4	2	3	3	4	3	2	3	3
N	1	5	1	6	1	9	1	6	1	5
Ñ	N/A	N/A	N/A	N/A	N/A	N/A	N/A	N/A	8	1
O	2	3	1	6	2	3	1	8	1	8
Ö	7	1	N/A	N/A	8	1	N/A	N/A	N/A	N/A
P	5	1	3	2	4	1	3	2	3	2
Q	N/A	N/A	8	1	10	1	10	1	8	1
R	1	6	1	6	1	6	1	6	1	4
RR	N/A	N/A	N/A	N/A	N/A	N/A	N/A	N/A	8	1
S	2	3	1	6	1	7	1	4	1	7
Ş	4	2	N/A	N/A	N/A	N/A	N/A	N/A	N/A	N/A
T	1	5	1	6	1	6	1	6	1	4
U	2	3	1	6	1	6	1	4	1	6
Ü	3	2	N/A	N/A	6	1	N/A	N/A	N/A	N/A
V	7	1	4	2	6	1	4	2	4	2
W	N/A	N/A	10	1	3	1	4	2	8	1
X	N/A	N/A	10	1	8	1	8	1	8	1
Y	3	2	10	1	10	1	4	2	4	2
Z	4	2	10	1	3	1	10	1	10	1
Blank	0	2	0	2	0	2	0	2	0	2
Total	N/A	100	N/A	102	N/A	102	N/A	100	N/A	100

Scrabble is available in a range of other languages, including: Hebrew, Greek, Arabic, Russian, Bulgarian, Catalan, Czech, Slovak, and Braille.

—HORSE RACING TRACK 'GOING' CONDITIONS—

DIRT TRACKS · USA
frozen · fast · good · wet-fast · sloppy · muddy · slow · heavy

TURF TRACKS · USA
firm · hard · soft · good · yielding

TURF TRACKS · UK
heavy · soft · good-to-soft · good · good-to-firm · firm · hard

ALL-WEATHER TRACKS · UK
fast · standard · slow

————————COMPULSIVE GAMBLING————————

Gamblers Anonymous use these questions to help gamblers beat their addiction. Most compulsive gamblers answer '*yes*' to at least 7 of them:

Do you lose time from work due to gambling?
Is gambling making your home life unhappy?
Is gambling affecting your reputation?
Have you ever felt remorse after gambling?
Do you ever gamble to get money with which to pay debts or to
otherwise solve financial difficulties?
Does gambling cause a decrease in your ambition or efficiency?
After losing, do you feel you must return as soon as possible
and win back your losses?
After a win do you have a strong urge to return and win more?
Do you often gamble until your last pound is gone?
Do you ever borrow to finance your gambling?
Have you ever sold anything to finance gambling?
Are you reluctant to use gambling money for normal expenditures?
Does gambling make you careless of the welfare of your family?
Do you gamble longer than you planned?
Do you ever gamble to escape worry or trouble?
Have you ever committed, or considered committing,
an illegal act to finance gambling?
Does gambling cause you to have difficulty in sleeping?
Do arguments, disappointments, or frustrations
create an urge within you to gamble?
Do you have an urge to celebrate any good fortune
by a few hours' gambling?
Have you ever considered self-destruction as a result of your gambling?

——ARCHAIC GOLF CLUB NOMENCLATURE——

Few formal links exist between modern and ancient golf clubs, but the list below gives an approximate guide to what comparisons can be made:

Woods No.1	Play Club, Driver	No.4	Jigger, Mashie Iron
No.2	Brassie	No.5	Mashie
No.3	Spoon	No.6	Spade Mashie
No.4	Baffy	No.7	Mashie-Niblick
		No.8	Pitching Mashie
Irons No.1	Driving Iron, Cleek	No.9	Niblick, Baffing Spoon
No.2	Cleek, Midiron	PW/SW	Wedge or Jigger
No.3	Mid-Mashie	Putter/Blank	Putter

The Brassie (or Brassy) was a wooden club with a head shod with brass. The Spoon had a slightly concave head that was handy for playing lofted shots to escape hollows. The Baffy was similarly employed for loft, being described as a short, stiff club with a 'laid back' face. Cleeks (or Cleques) were long-shafted narrow-faced clubs used for distance. The Mashie was a standard club used for medium distance and loft – probably deriving its name from an ancient term for a war-hammer. The Niblick was originally a wooden club, later manufactured as a lofted iron with a short face. It has been suggested that the word Niblick might be a corruption of the Scottish term for a broken nose – *neb laigh*. During the 1971 Apollo 14 mission, Alan Shepard fitted an 8-iron head (equivalent to a pitching mashie) to a 'lunar sample collection device' and hit two golf balls on the Moon. Since 1939, the maximum number of clubs a player is permitted in their bag is 14. This rule cost Ian Woosnam a two-shot penalty when his caddie Miles Byrne left a 15th club – a test driver – in Woosnam's bag during the 2001 Open at Royal Lytham & St Anne's.

——— SOME FLY-FISHING LURES OF NOTE ———

The best fly-fishermen like nothing better than to fashion their own lures to entrap fish. Some of the more elaborate traditional lures are below:

The butcher... *red tail feather, black cock hackle[†], crow quill feather wings*
Black Zulu[*] .... *black ostrich & silver tinsel body, black cock hackle*
Welsh partridge .... *claret seal's fur body, dark partridge feather tail*
Silver blue... *silver tinsel body, blue peacock hackle, dyed-blue feather wings*
Sweep .... *black henny cock hackle, black wings, bluefisher feather cheeks*
Coalman.......... *black wool body, teal feather wings, golden pheasant tail*
Pot scrubber .... *copper pot scrubber body, gray squirrel fur wings*
Orange peril .. *orange & green marabou tail, gold tinsel body, orange wings*
Dogstail ...... *beige dog hair tied with brown silk body, reddish cock hackle*
Snipe & purple ..... *purple silk body, black hackle from a jack snipe's wing*

[†]Hackles (or palmers) are made from long neck feathers and are used to alter buoyancy.
[*]Black Zulu lures were at one time prohibited from competitive angling as too efficient.

SOME F1 CIRCUITS OF NOTE

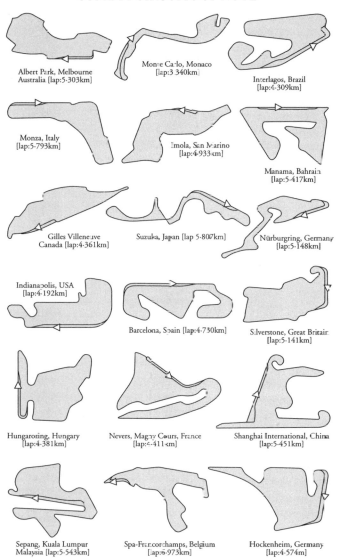

Albert Park, Melbourne
Australia [lap:5·303km]

Monte Carlo, Monaco
[lap:3·340km]

Interlagos, Brazil
[lap:4·309km]

Monza, Italy
[lap:5·793km]

Imola, San Marino
[lap:4·933km]

Manama, Bahrain
[lap:5·417km]

Gilles Villeneuve
Canada [lap:4·361km]

Suzuka, Japan [lap 5·807km]

Nürburgring, Germany
[lap:5·148km]

Indianapolis, USA
[lap:4·192km]

Barcelona, Spain [lap:4·730km]

Silverstone, Great Britain
[lap:5·141km]

Hungaroring, Hungary
[lap:4·381km]

Nevers, Magny Cours, France
[lap:4·411km]

Shanghai International, China
[lap:5·451km]

Sepang, Kuala Lumpur
Malaysia [lap:5·543km]

Spa-Francorchamps, Belgium
[lap:6·973km]

Hockenheim, Germany
[lap:4·574m]

———— GREYHOUND TRAP COLOR CODING ————

	Red	Pink	White	Black	Orange	Black & White	Yellow	Blue	Green	Green & White	Yellow & Black	Purple
Great Britain	1		3	4	5	6		2				
Australia	1	8	3	7			2	5	4	6		
Ireland	1		3	4	5	6		2				
Spain	1		3	4	5	6		2				
USA	1		3	5			6	2	4	7	8	9

———— SCHEMATICS OF CROQUET HOOP ORDER ————

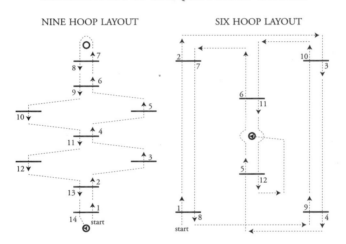

NINE HOOP LAYOUT   SIX HOOP LAYOUT

———————— BOLÉRO ————————

Originally of Moroccan origin, the *boléro* was introduced to Spain by Sebastian Zerezo in *c.*1780, and it was quickly adopted as the Spanish national dance. The *boléro* is in 2/4 or 3/4 time resembling the fandango. Maurice Ravel's one-act ballet crescendo *Boléro* (1928) is certainly the most famous example of the dance – in part because it was used in the film *10* where Dudley Moore falls in lust with Bo Derek, but certainly because it was interpreted by Jayne Torvill and Christopher Dean when they won Gold in the 1984 Winter Olympics ice dance. The pair scored 3 × 6·0 and 6 × 5·9 for *technical skill*, and 9 × 6·0 for *artistic impression*.

—— FRAUDS' INTERPRETATION OF DREAMS ——

Oneiromancy – divination by the interpretation of dreams – has long preoccupied mankind. Below are some oneiromantic interpretations from a variety of (frankly dubious) Victorian and Edwardian 'dream guides':

Subject of dream   *denotes*

Alphabet	success through one's own efforts
Ants	one's industry will be rewarded
Bagpipes; bagpipe music	sadness; loss of a loved one
Beavers	danger from hidden enemies
Candles	[lit] pleasing correspondence awaits; [unlit] sickness
Chimney sweeps	excellent fortune ahead
Coffin with flowers	a sick friend will recover
Dancing	good news will come from a long-absent friend
Drowning	financial difficulties await
Earwigs	the risk of persecution or prosecution
Elephants	good fortune; wisdom; new friendships
Finding objects	anxiety about losing something
Frogs	one should be suspicious of strangers or foreigners
Gallows	excellent luck and financial prosperity
Gloves	honor and safety; [torn] disrupted friendship
Hail	grief and sorrow; troubles to be overcome with perseverance
Horseshoes	good luck; a happy home
Ice	great responsibility; plentiful harvest
Jury	disappointment; the need for assistance
Keys	[found] riches and wealth; [lost] disappointment
Kites	a quarrel with friends or relations; uncertainty
Labyrinths	distress; confusion; troubles caused by money or relatives
Lawyers	distress and anguish
Midwives	the revealing of hitherto well-kept secrets
Nails	work, industry, labor; moderate fortune and success
Oranges	misfortune; loss of goods and reputation
Ostriches	trouble through the envy of others
Packages	imminent receipt of a gift or present; fear of change
Peaches	good fortune; success in friendship, business, and love
Queen	imminent good news; fortune in love and romance
Railway	news or a visit from a long-absent friend
Shadow	cares and troubles; [your own] loss, poverty, old age
Squirrels	a prosperous marriage or business alliance; contentment
Tea-pot	new friendship
Urn	[empty] death; [broken] disputes; [with ashes] inheritance
Volcano	bad news; change and uncertainty; family disputes
Wine	happiness; good fortune; festivities
Zebra	the spite of previously trusted friends

─────── GEORGE ORWELL ON THE LOTTERY ───────

The Lottery, with its weekly pay-out of enormous prizes, was the one public event to which the proles paid serious attention. It was probable that there were some millions of proles for whom the Lottery was the principal if not the only reason for remaining alive. It was their delight, their folly, their anodyne, their intellectual stimulant. Where the Lottery was concerned, even people who could barely read and write seemed capable of intricate calculations and staggering feats of memory.

— GEORGE ORWELL, *Nineteen Eighty-Four*, 1949

─────────── NORWAY & IDLING ───────────

According to the lastest figures from the Organization for Economic Co-peration and Developement (OECD) Norway is the ideal country to move to if you're idle. There the 'average hours worked' per-year per-person in work is 1,337 – compared to 1,792 in the US, and 2,390 in Korea:

country	hours	± USA
United States	1,792	—
Australia	1,814	+22
Canada	1,718	−74
Denmark	1,475	−317
France	1,431	−361
Germany	1,446	−346
Greece	1,938	+146
Ireland	1,613	−179
Italy	1,591	−201
Japan	1,801	+9
Korea	2,390	+598
Mexico	1,857	+65
Netherlands	1,354	−438
Norway	1,337	−455
United Kingdom	1,673	−119

Norway

Oslo ★

OECD Factbook 2005

────── THE QUALITIES OF A GOOD GREYHOUND ──────

A greyhound should be *heeded* lyke a SNAKE,
And *necked* lyke a DRAKE, *Backed* lyke a BREAM,
Footed lyke a CATTE, *Taylled* lyke a RATTE.

— JULIANA BERNERS, *Book of St Albans*, 1486

AGAINST FOOTBALL

A devilishe pastime ... and hereof groweth envy, rancour, and malice, and sometimes brawling, murder, homicide, and great effusion of blood.

— PHILIP STUBBES, *Anatomie of Abuses*, 1583

THE FIRST NEWSPAPER CROSSWORD

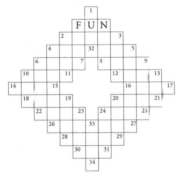

It is thought that the first ever published crossword was this one devised in 1913 by Liverpudlian Arthur Wynne for the American Sunday newspaper the *New York World*. After initial doubts and some experimentation with the diamond shape, the now-familiar square crossword became firmly established. In 1924 the *Sunday Express* printed the UK's first newspaper crossword, and in 1930, *The Times* followed suit.

2–3 ... *What bargain hunters enjoy*
6–22........ *What we all should be*
4–5 .... *A written acknowledgment*
4–26 .... *A day dream*
6–7 .... *Such and nothing more*
2–11 .... *A talon*
10–11....................... *A bird*
19–28.................... *A pigeon*
14–15............... *Opposed to less*
F–7.............. *Part of your head*
18–19.......... *What this puzzle is*
23–30............ *A river in Russia*
22–23 .... *An animal of prey*
1–32 .... *To govern*
26–27........... *The close of a day*
33–34 .... *An aromatic plant*

28–29 .... *To elude*
N–8 .... *A fist*
30–31 .... *The plural of is*
24–31 .... *To agree with*
8–9.................... *To cultivate*
3–12 .... *Part of a ship*
12–13....... *A bar of wood or iron*
20–29 .... *One*
16–17 ..... *What artists learn to do*
5–27 .... *Exchanging*
20–21.................... *Fastened*
9–25 .... *To sink in mud*
24–25 .... *Found on the seashore*
13–21....................... *A boy*
10–18 *The fiber of the gomuti palm*
[The solution can be found on p.160.]

GOLF GRAND-SLAM EVENTS

Masters (April) · US Open (June) · British Open (July) · PGA (August)

CHESS NOTATION

Although a number of different systems of chess notations exist, perhaps the most useful is the Algebraic System. Here, pieces are indicated by these prefixed letters:

K = king · Q = queen · R = rook
B = bishop · N = knight
(pawns are identified by having no prefix)

The eight Ranks and Files are identified with numbers and letters *(as in the diagram opposite)*.

Consequently, each square has a unique designator, from a8 in the top left-hand corner, to h1 in the bottom right. The moves made by pieces are indicated by the prefixed letter followed by the square of *arrival* (when pawns are moved, only the square of arrival is noted). If a piece captures another, the letter x is inserted before the square of arrival, for example: Rxd1. When a pawn captures a piece, the file of departure is added before the x and the square of arrival, for example: gxf3. If a pawn is promoted, the move is indicated as normal but the prefix letter of its new identity is added, for example: f8Q. (Other conventions exist for such circumstances as when two identical pieces can move to the same square, and so on.) In addition, a range of other abbreviations are used to describe play, such as:

+ . . . . check	? . . . . bad move
++ . . . . checkmate	?? . . . . serious mistake
0-0 . . . . Kingside castling	(?) . . . . questionable move
0-0-0 . . . . Queenside castling	!? . . . . interesting, risky move
e.p. . . . . captures *en passant*	?! . . . . dubious, very risky move
1-0 . . . . Black resigns (White wins)	! . . . . good move
0-1 . . . . White resigns (Black wins)	!! . . . . brilliant move
½-½ or = ... draw agreed	⊙ . . . . zugzwang

REGAL SPORTS & LOVE

I know how to perform eight exercises: I fight with courage; I keep a firm seat on horseback; I am skilled in swimming; I glide along the ice on skates; I excel in darting the lance; I am dexterous at the oar; and yet a Russian maid disdains me.

— HAROLD II (1022–66) [attrib.]

—————————SOME NOTABLE SLEEPERS—————————

❧ The Greek poet EPIMENIDES is said to have fallen asleep in a cave as a child, and not to have awoken for fifty-seven years, after which he found himself possessed of all wisdom. ❧ In Washington Irving's 1819 story RIP VAN WINKLE slept for twenty years in the Catskill Mountains, waking an old man, 'unknowing and unknown'. ❧ Arthurian legend tells of MERLIN, who is not dead, but asleep in the form of an old tree yet to wake; and KING ARTHUR himself, who is not dead in Avalon, but is sleeping in the form of a raven. (Incidentally, some say that Merlin was responsible for waking ST DAVID, who was enchanted into sleep for seven years by Ormandine.) ❧ DOG SLEEP, CAT SLEEP, FOX SLEEP, and WEASEL SLEEP are all feigned sleeps taken with one eye metaphorically open. ❧ German mythology tells of CHARLES V, who is asleep until it is time to awake and reclaim his monarchy, and BARBAROSSA, who sleeps with six knights until they are ready to awake and establish Germany as the most powerful state on Earth. ❧ It is said that ST EUTHYMUS slept standing against a wall, and ARSENUS hardly slept at all. ❧ MARGARET THATCHER famously thrived on three or four hours' sleep a night, as did NAPOLEON and the Chinese Communist ZHOU ENLAI. BENJAMIN FRANKLIN once declared: 'Up, sluggard, and waste not life; in the grave will be sleeping enough'. In contrast, HAROLD WILSON said, 'I believe the greatest asset a head of state can have is the ability to get a good night's sleep'. ❧ The SEVEN SLEEPERS OF EPHESUS were persecuted Christians who sought refuge in a cave at the time of the Emperor Decius (AD250), and slept for 200 years. They awoke in AD447 during the reign of Theodosius II. ❧ The story of SLEEPING BEAUTY, popularized by Charles Perrault (1628–1703), tells of a beautiful princess cursed by a wicked fairy to prick her finger and die. Fortunately, a good fairy commutes this death sentence into sleep lasting 100 years, from which the princess is released by the kiss of a handsome prince. ❧ Irish legend tells of DESMOND OF KILMALLOCK, who is not dead but asleep in the icy waters of Lough Gur, Limerick. It is said that once each year Desmond awakes and rides in full armor around the Lough before returning to his deep slumber. ❧ A SLEEPLESS HAT is one that is so worn-out it has no nap. ❧ It is said that CHARLEMAGNE is not dead but asleep near Salzburg, waiting for the rise of the Antichrist, at which time he will awaken, conquer evil, and herald the return of Christ. ❧ In Greek mythology, ENDYMION was a handsome shepherd who, while tending flocks on Mount Latmos one night, was spotted sleeping naked by the moon-goddess Selene. Instantly falling in love, Selene flew to Earth in a chariot of silver, and made sweet, sweet love with him. Becoming jealous of his beauty, Selene kissed Endymion's eyes and condemned him to a dreamless sleep during which he would never age. ❧ MORPHEUS is the god of dreams (the son of Somnus, or Hypnos, the ancient god of sleep), after whom the narcotic morphine is named. ❧

—— CLASSIC POKER-HAND NICKNAMES ——

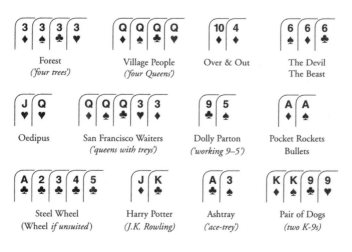

The AK47
Machine Gun

Magnum
(Colt .44)

Motown
('Jacks-on-fives')

The Horsemen
(of the Apocalypse)

James Butler 'Wild Bill' Hickok was a stockman, soldier, spy, deputy US marshall, murderer, sheriff of Ellis County, Ka., marshall of Abilene, Ka., and holder of the most famous hand in poker. When he was shot dead by Jack McCall on 2 August 1876, Wild Bill was holding two black Aces and two black 8s – ever after known as DEADMAN'S HAND. As might be expected from such a legend, considerable dispute surrounds the composition of Hickok's hand, especially the identity of the fifth card or 'kicker'. Most sources agree that the 'kicker' was the 8 of Hearts, but others assert the Jack of Spades, the 9 of Diamonds (see p.54), or even the Queen of Spades.

Forest
('four trees')

Village People
('four Queens')

Over & Out

The Devil
The Beast

Oedipus

San Francisco Waiters
('queens with treys')

Dolly Parton
('working 9–5')

Pocket Rockets
Bullets

Steel Wheel
(Wheel *if unsuited*)

Harry Potter
(J.K. Rowling)

Ashtray
('ace-trey')

Pair of Dogs
(two K-9s)

————————— PLUS-FOURS —————————

Plus-fours are the knicker(bocker)s traditionally favored by golfers, so named because four extra inches of material were added so that they hung down below the knee. Plus-sixes, plus-eights, and even plus-tens were occasionally sported, though these tended to hinder the follow-through.

BACK TO SQUARE ONE

It is possible that the expression 'back to square one' has its origin in the early days of BBC radio football commentary. In order to help listeners at home follow the live commentary, the *Radio Times* printed a schematic of the pitch subdivided into 8 squares (see below). When the ball was passed towards the goal-keeper it went back to square one. The first match to use this diagram was Arsenal *vs* Sheffield, at Highbury, on 22 January 1927.

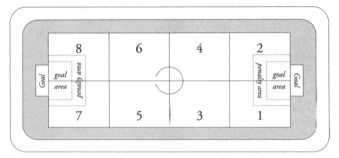

An alternative derivation is that the phrase comes from *Snakes & Ladders*.

THE HOLLYWOOD CRICKET CLUB

The Hollywood Cricket Club was the brainchild of Charles 'Round the Corner' Aubrey Smith (1863–1948) – a right-handed fast bowler who captained England on the 1888–9 tour of South Africa, and was knighted for services to Anglo-American cordiality in 1944. (His nickname derived from a highly idiosyncratic bowling approach, described by W.G. Grace as 'startling'.) Smith was also a Hollywood actor who starred in over 100 pictures, including *Rebecca* (1940) and *Little Women* (1949) – though he tended to be typecast as the archetypal Englishman and even managed to portray the Duke of Wellington in three different films. In 1932, when Smith was living near Mulholland Drive, he persuaded the Los Angeles Park Commission to donate some land on which to build a cricket pitch. Grass seed was imported from England, a pavilion was constructed, and the Aubrey Smith Cricket Field quickly became a mecca for American and ex-pat cricketers. An impressive roll-call of names gained membership in the Club, including Douglas Fairbanks Jr., Cary Grant, David Niven, Basil Rathbone, H.B. Warner, P.G. Wodehouse, Ronald Coleman, and Nigel Bruce – though Smith was not shy in pressurising players to attend. Laurence Olivier was once summoned by note to attend a practice and turned up at nets wearing boots he had borrowed from Boris Karloff.

—————————— THE ART OF BULLFIGHTING ——————————

Bullfighting is the only art in which the artist is in danger of death and in which the degree of brilliance in the performance is left to the fighter's honor.

— ERNEST HEMINGWAY, *Death in the Afternoon*, 1932

—————————— RACKING OF POOL BALLS ——————————

BLACKBALL

15 balls are racked in a triangle. The black ball is placed in the center, and the remaining red and yellow balls are arranged as shown in the diagram below:

9 BALL

9 balls are racked in a diamond formation with the 1-ball at the top, the 9-ball in the center, and the remaining balls in a random order. For example:

US 8 BALL

15 balls are racked with the 8-ball in the center, as below. A stripe must be in one bottom corner, and a solid in the other. The rest are randomly placed. For example:

[The UK version of BLACKBALL is called UK 8 BALL and has slightly different racking.]

—————————— 'SPOOF' ——————————

Spoof is a classic drinking game of cunning, deception, and guile where the aim is to be eliminated as quickly as possible. Any number of players sit round a table and surreptitiously place between 0 and 3 coins in one of their hands. When instructed, all place their fist onto the table in front of them. Then, the participants take it in turn to guess the *total* number of coins held in *all* of the hands (usually, the tallest guesses first, and the guessing then rotates counter-clockwise). In a group of five players, for example, the guesses can range between 0 and 15. Importantly, no one may guess the same figure as another. When all have guessed, the coins are revealed and the player who has correctly estimated the total drops out. The game continues until there is only one player left – the loser.

————————— FORMULA 1 PIT CREW —————————

[a] fire-extinguisher man · [b] rear jack man · [c] wheel on · [d] gun man · [e] wheel off & starter motor · [f] dead man's handle · [g] exhaust-shield man · [h] hose support · [i] fuel-nozzle man · [j] rig programmer · [k] rad-duct cleaner · [l] wheel off · [m] gun man · [n] wheel on & front wing adjuster · [o] front jack man · [p] lollipop man · [q] wheel on & front wing adjuster · [r] gun man · [s] wheel off · [t] visor cleaner & rad-duct cleaner · [u] car steady · [v] wheel on · [w] gun man · [x] wheel off

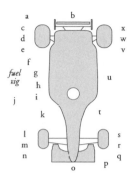

————————— ACTIVITY AT ALTITUDE —————————

Activity	meters ± sea-level
Highest recorded skydive (in pressurized suit)	31,334
Highest point reached by balloonist in pressurized capsule	19,811
Human blood boils	$c.$19,000
Highest a human can go breathing pure oxygen	$c.$12,000
Peak of Everest, highest point on Earth	8,850
Mt Aucanquilcha Mine, highest permanent human settlement	5,340
Hernando Siles Stadium, La Paz, Bolivia	3,600
Azteca Stadium, Mexico City	2,240
World record pole vault	6·14
World's lowest golf course, Furnace Creek, Death Valley, USA	-65
Depths reached by freedivers	$c.$-72
Depths reached by freedivers using weights	-160
Deepest scuba dive	$c.$-313
Depth humans can reach with special equipment	-450
Depth reached by diving elephant seals	-1,500
Krubera Cave, Georgia, deepest cave explored by pot-holers	-1,710
Challenger Deep, Marianas Trench, deepest point in the world	-10,915

On 15 April 1875, H.T. Sivel, Gaston Tissandier, and J.E Croce-Spinelli took off from outside Paris in the balloon *Zenith* to study the effects of altitude. When the balloon reached 8,000m all three were overcome with hypoxia and fainted before they could use the onboard supply of oxygen. As they flickered in and out of consciousness, the three aviators became increasingly confused and mistakenly let fall more ballast, causing them to rise even higher. Tissandier finally woke when the balloon descended to 6,000m, by which time both his companions were dead.

———————— THE PALIO OF SIENA ————————

Twice a year, in July and August, ten horses are raced bareback three times around the *Piazza del Campo* in the Italian city of Siena. The race itself lasts only 90 seconds – a fleeting duration which belies the history, pride, and passion that suffuse the event. The contest is known as the *Palio* – which is also the name of the silk standard for which the race is run. *Palios* have taken place in Siena since at least 1238, and only seismic events like cholera, earthquakes, rioting, and war have been allowed to interfere. (Although, in 1919, when rioting was sweeping across the rest of Italy, Siena was curiously peaceful during the *Palio* season.) The key to the *Palio* lies in the structure of Siena, which is divided into *contrade* that act as small social, political, and (historically) military units. In the C14th there were at least 42 *contrade*, but since 1729 there have been just 17:

The division of Siena into its 17 contrade (the numbers correspond to the table opposite); and a schematic of the Piazza del Campo, showing the direction taken by the Palio riders.

The *contrade* are defined by well-established (though invisible) borders which criss-cross the city – each has its own government, motto, saint, emblem, colors, museum, lucky number, and so on. The pride of a *contrada* depends absolutely upon the outcome of each *Palio*. To win a race brings honor and delight; to lose, shame and sadness. Indeed, to come second is considered a far greater humiliation than coming last. Furthermore, a *contrada* allied to the winner will share in its victory; and the winning *contrada's* traditional rival will be considered to have lost, even if they did not race. It is hard to overstate the complexity of the *Palio*, every facet of which is charged with tradition, superstition, and competitive suspicion from selecting which ten *contrade* will race, to allocating each *contrada* a horse. Before each race every horse is taken by its *contrada* into their church to be blessed, after which the horses are carefully guarded to prevent attack from rival *contrade*. During the race itself the jockeys *(fatini)* hold no quarter in intimidating the competition, not least with their *nerbo* – 2½-foot-long whips made from the stretched phalluses of unweaned calves. Once the race is over, the crowds that packed every spare foot of the Piazza mob the winning jockey and horse, scrambling to touch the silk *Palio* itself. This signals the commencement of the celebrations and commiserations which then engulf Siena for days.

The pride of *contrada* membership is fierce and, just as some Yorkshiremen would insist their sons be born in the county to ensure their eligibility for the Yorkshire cricket team, so many Sienese would travel across Italy so that their children might be born in the correct *contrada*. Tabulated below are some of the distinctive features of each of the seventeen *contrade*:

Name	Translation	Associated trade	Colors	Saint's Day	Rivals	Allies	Motto	Wins
1..AQUILA†	*eagle*	notaries	y-lb-bla	Sep 8	13	5,4	From the eagle, beak, claw, and wing	24
2....BRUCO†	*caterpillar*	silk workers	y-lb-g	Jul 2		7,10,16	My name rings out like a revolution	35
3..CHIOCCIOLA	*snail*	tanners	y-t-r	Jun 29	15	7,13,14	Slowly and surely will the Snail win	50
4...CIVETTA	*owl*	cobblers	bla-r-w	Jun 13	8	1,6,7,13	I see through the night	32
5...DRAGO	*dragon*	bankers	r-y-g	Apr 29		1	Fire in my heart becomes flame in my mouth	36
6...GIRAFFA	*giraffe*	painters	w-r	July		4,7,13	The higher the head, the greater the glory	33
7...ISTRICE	*porcupine*	smiths	w-r-bla-lbl	Aug 24	9	?,3,4,6	I prick out of defence	40
8...LEOCORNO	*unicorn*	goldsmiths	w-o-r	Jun 24	4	13,15	The arm I bear wounds and heals equally	28
9...LUPA	*she-wolf*	bakers	o-bla-w	Aug 16	7		Et urbis et senarum signum et decus	34
10..NICCHIO†	*shell*	potters	lb-y-r	Aug 7	17	2,12,15	The red of the coral burns in my heart	42
11..OCA†	*goose*	dyers	w-g-r	Apr 29	16		Clangit ad arma	61
12..ONDA	*wave*	carpenters	w.lb	Jul 2	16	10,15,17	The color of sky, the strength of ocean	37.5
13..PANTERA	*panther*	apothecaries	r w-lb	Aug 29	1	3,4,6,8	The panther roared, the people were afraid	25
14..SELVA	*forest*	weavers	g-o-w	Aug 15		3,15	The first forest in the Campo	33
15..TARTUCA	*tortoise*	stonemasons	y-t	Jun 13	3	8,10,12,14	Strength and consistency	44.5
16..TORRE	*tower*	wool carders	r-w-lb	Jul 25	11,12	2	Alongside strength, power	43
17..MONTONE	*ram*	silk merchants	r-y-w	Apr 26	10	12	Walls crumble under my horns	43

Contrade have only been numbered to facilitate identification of allied and rival contrada, and for the map opposite. · Number of wins, as of 2004.

Color code: Red, Light Blue, Dark Blue, Yellow, White, Green, Black, Turquoise, Orange, Blue, Pink

†*Indicates one of the 'Noble Contrade'; so called because of royal recognition*

———— SLEEP AND ITS STAGES ————

Sleep is generally accepted to be an easily reversed, regular, and natural period of partial or complete unconsciousness, during which the activity of the nervous system is to some degree suspended, the body rests and recuperates, and the individual's responsiveness to their environment is diminished. Although it was long believed that sleep was not uniform, only with the development of the electroencephalogram (EEG), and other electrical tests, were the two main phases or stages of sleep identified:

Non-Rapid-Eye Movement [NREM] sleep has four stages of successive depth *(see the EEG traces opposite)*. It is characterized by a reduction in brain activity, metabolic rate, heart rate, blood-pressure, temperature, and so on. It is thought that NREM sleep is important for growth, energy conservation, and possibly for processing information that was acquired during wakefulness.

Rapid-Eye Movement [REM] sleep is characterized by a reduction in muscle tone, mild involuntary muscle jerks, and the presence of rapid eye movements. REM is the phase when most dreaming takes place, and brain activity increases. In adults, 20–30% of sleep is REM sleep. The function and meaning of dreams are disputed (see p.77).

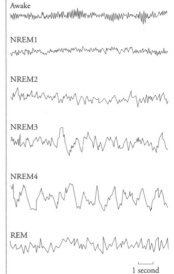

Awake

NREM1

NREM2

NREM3

NREM4

REM

⊢——⊣
1 second

Most sleep begins with NREM1 which lasts roughly 30sec–7min, after which NREM2 takes over, and NREM3 & 4 then occur within 45min or so. Before the first phase of REM we usually return briefly to NREM2. We then tend to alternate between NREM & REM sleep around 4–5 times, at intervals of about 90min; with each alternation the REM period is longer and more intense, and our final sleep stages tend to be NREM2 & REM.

———— GYMNASTICS EVENTS ————

MEN · *floor* · *vault* · *pommel-horse* · *parallel bars* · *horizontal bar* · *rings*
WOMEN · *floor exercises* · *vault* · *balance beam* · *asymmetrical bars*

--------------------------- GOT SPORT? ---------------------------

Some of those athletes who have sported the 'Got Milk?' milk mustache:

Andy Roddick [tennis] · Amy Van Dyken [swimmer] · Andre Agassi [tennis]
Brad Johnson [football] · Ekaterina Gordeeva [ice skater]
Jason Kidd [point guard] · Lara Croft [tomb raider] · Cal Ripken Jr. [baseball]
Jeff Gordon [NASCAR driver] · 'Pistol' Pete Sampras [tennis]
Marion Jones [track & field] · Mark McGwire [baseball]
Mat Hoffman [BMX biker] · Oscar de la Hoya [boxer]
'Stone Cold' Steve Austin [wrestler] · Terrell Davis [football]
Tony Hawk [skateboarder] · Tony Meola [soccer] · Ty Law [football]
Serena & Venus Williams [tennis] · Zhang Ziyi [crouching tiger]
Arie Luyendyk [racing driver] · Muhammad Ali [boxer] ·
Kristi Yamaguchi [ice skater] · Austin Powers [nternational man of mystery]
Michael Johnson [runner] · Florence G Joyner [runner]

--------------- ON THE NOISES OF HORSES ---------------

A *snort* is a danger signal to the whole herd; a *neigh* is a distress call; a *nicker* is a sign of relief; and a *whinny* is a call of pleasure and expectancy.

— M.E. ENSMINGER, *The Complete Encyclopedia of Horses*, 1977

--------------- JAMES BOND vs HUGO DRAX ---------------

In Ian Fleming's novel *Moonraker* (1955), Sir Hugo Drax is suspected of cheating at bridge in the exclusive Mayfair club Blades. James Bond is called in by M to see whether these suspicions are true since, as M warns, 'cheating at cards can still smash a man. In so-called Society, it's about the only crime that can still finish you'. Bond quickly ascertains that Drax is indeed a cheat who places his silver cigarette-case on the baize to act as a 'Shiner' reflecting the cards as he

	BOND	
	♦ Q, 8, 7, 6, 5, 4, 3, 2	
	♣ A, Q, 10, 8, 4	
DRAX		MEYER
♠ A, K, Q, J		♠ 6, 5, 4, 3, 2
♥ A, K, Q, J		♥ 10, 9, 8, 7, 2
♦ A, K		♦ J, 10, 9
♣ K, J, 9		
	M	
	♠ 10, 9, 8, 7	
	♥ 6, 5, 4, 3	
	♣ 7, 6, 5, 3, 2	

deals. Bond decides to humiliate Drax by switching the packs and dealing a rigged hand. Bond credits the hand to the bridge player Ely Culbertson (1891–1955), though it is probably a version of the famous whist hand which lost the Duke of Cumberland (1721–65) a reported bet of £20,000.

KARATE BELTS

The use of colored belts to denote experience and status is common to many martial arts, though the exact color coding varies both across and within disciplines. The convention that the belts get darker as the wearer becomes more qualified has been explained in a number of ways. Some say it is because traditionally the belts were never washed and therefore discolored with age; others say that the belts were kept and dyed anew. Below is one of the many color schemes, this one from Shotokan Karate:

Grade	Belt	Japanese
10th Kyu	white	*Soshinsha*
9th Kyu	orange	*Kukyu*
8th Kyu	red	*Hachikyu*
7th Kyu	yellow	*Shichikyu*
6th Kyu	green	*Rokkyu*
5th Kyu	purple	*Gokyu*
4th Kyu	purple & white	*Yonkyu*
3rd Kyu	brown	*Sankyu*
2nd Kyu	brown & white	*Nikyu*
1st Kyu	brown & white	*Ikkyu*
1st Dan	black	*Shodan*
2nd Dan	black	*Nidan*
3rd Dan	black	*Sandan*
4th Dan	black	*Yondan*
5th Dan	black	*Godan*
6th Dan	black	*Rokudan*
7th Dan	black	*Shichidan*
8th Dan	black	*Hachidan*
9th Dan	black	*Kudan*
10th Dan	black	*Judan*

ON WOMEN AND CYCLING

Only a few years ago bicycling was looked upon as a past-time quite unsuited to women. The tricycle was used by a few who felt they needed more vigorous exercise than could be obtained by walking or playing a quiet game of croquet ... But now there is a reaction in its favour and only a few of the obstinately blind are found in opposition ... There is no doubt that the bicycle has brought health to many a nervous, over-wrought woman. All depends, of course, on the common sense displayed by the individual ... No woman should ride if she has any serious weakness, except with great caution, and the permission of a doctor who not only understands her constitution, but who has also made a special study of cycling in all its phases.

— SUSAN, COUNTESS OF MALMESBURY, 1897

TENNIS GRAND-SLAM, SURFACES, & MONTHS

Australian Open *(Rebound Ace)* [Jan] · French Open *(red clay)* [May/Jun]
Wimbledon *(grass)* [Jun/Jul] · US Open *(cement)* [Aug/Sep]

— 'KABADDI-KABADDI-KABADDI-KABADDI' —

A cross between 'It' and 'British Bulldog', *Kabaddi* is almost certainly the only non-aquatic sport where the ability to hold one's breath is essential. Although the game has a set of well-ordered rules and regulations, some of which are detailed below, the essence of *Kabaddi* is that it can be played almost anywhere, by any group, with no specialist clothing or equipment.

Formal *Kabaddi* courts are 13m × 10m, divided into two halves, each of which is again divided ⅔rds along by *baulk* lines. Because each side fields only 7 players out of a squad of 12, *sitting blocks* are positioned at either end of the court.

Teams take it in turns to send a *raider* into the opposing team's half which is populated by the *anti-raiders* (or *antis*). Before crossing the center line, the *raiders* must loudly and clearly start to repeat the word *Kabaddi*† (over and over again) to demonstrate that they are not breathing in. This repetition is known as the *cant*, and any player who pauses during his *cant* is out. (Players are also out if they cross the court's boundary lines.) Once within the opposing team's half, *raiders* attempt to cross their opponent's *baulk* line and then return home while touching as many of the *antis* as possible. If a *raider* manages this while keeping his *cant* going it is known as a *successful raid*, and all those *antis* who were touched during the *raid* are ruled out. It is the job of the *antis* to *hold* the *raider* and prevent him from returning to his court before his *cant* collapses. Any *raider* who is *held* can get safe if he is able to touch the gound in his home half with any part of his body. When a player is out he must leave the field, and is only *revived* when a member of the opposing team gets out‡. Teams score 1 point for each player they put out, and 2 bonus points (a *lona*) for putting out an entire team. A typical games lasts 40 minutes with a 5-minute interval at half time; games are staged on weight and age categories. 7 officials police the game of *Kabaddi*, which is also played in a circular arena, when it becomes known as *Amar Kabaddi*.

† Kabaddi has been played under a host of other names that sometimes serve as the basis of the *cant*, including: *do-do-do, zabar gagana, hututu, chedu-gudu, kapati,* and *wandikali*.
‡ A number of variants have different rules for players given out: *sanjeevani*, where, once out, a player can be revived; *amar*, where a player given out can remain on the field, although his out is scored; and *ganimi*, where, once given out, a player cannot be revived.

—————— LAZY MAN'S LOAD ——————

A *Lazy Man's Load* is one too heavy to be carried; named after indolent types who overload themselves, hoping that they will not need to return.

GOLF IRON LOFT ANGLES

Below are illustrated the standard loft angles of a set of golf irons, along with the average range of male players, female players, and Tiger Woods:

Iron number	2	3	4	5	6	7	8	9	PW	SW
Face angle (c.)	20°	23°	26°	30°	34°	38°	42°	46°	50°	56°
Male (yds)	170-90	160-80	150-70	140-60	130-50	120-40	110-30	100-20	90-110	<100
Female (yds)	150-70	140-60	130-50	120-40	110-30	100-20	90-110	80-100	70-90	<80
Tiger (yds)	245	230	220	210	190	170	160	145	130	110

CHESTERFIELD ON LAZY & TRIFLING MINDS

Below is the distinction that Lord Chesterfield (1694–1773) made (on 26 July 1748) between LAZY and TRIFLING minds in one of the many authoritarian letters of instruction[†] he wrote to his illegitimate son Philip.

'The LAZY MIND will not take the trouble of going to the bottom of anything; but, discouraged by the first difficulties … stops short, contents itself with easy, and consequently superficial knowledge, and prefers a great degree of ignorance to a small degree of trouble …'

'The TRIFLING AND FRIVOLOUS mind is always busied, but to little purpose; it takes little objects for great ones, and throws away upon trifles that time and attention which only important things deserve. Knick-knacks; butterflies; shells, insects, etc., are the subjects of their most serious researches …'

'…For God's sake then reflect. Will you throw this time away either in laziness, or in trifles? … Read only useful books; and never quit a subject till you are thoroughly master of it, but read and inquire on till then.'

† *Samuel Johnson declared of Chesterfield's letters: 'They teach the morals of a whore, and the manners of a dancing master.' This barbed comment was provoked by Chesterfield's failure to live up to his offer of financial patronage while Johnson was compiling his* Dictionary of the English Language. *Johnson took further revenge by defining the word* patron *in his dictionary thus: 'Commonly a wretch who supports with insolence, and is paid with flattery'.*

HANDS, FEET, & HORSES

A HAND is the traditional measure of horses. In the C19th, a HAND was taken as 3 inches (¼ foot), but nowadays 4 inches (⅓ foot) is standard.

———————————— THE HAKA ————————————

Many different types of *Haka* exist – and most Maori tribes have their own variation, some performed with weapons, others without. The *Haka* famously performed by the New Zealand Rugby team is called *Ka Mate*.

An introduction by the leader reminds the team how to conduct the Haka:

Ringa pakia	Slap your thighs
Uma tiraha	Puff out the chest
Turi Whatia	Bend the knees
Hope whai ake	Let the hip follow
Waewae takahia kia kino	Stamp the feet as hard as you can

The whole team then performs:

Ka mate! Ka mate!	It is death! It is death!
Ka ora! Ka ora!	It is life! It is life!
Ka mate! Ka mate!	It is death! It is death!
Ka ora! Ka ora!	It is life! It is life!
Tenei te tangata puhuru huru	This is the man above me
Nana i tiki mai	Who enabled me to live
Whakawhiti te ra	As I climb up
A hupane, kaupane	Step by step
A hupane, kaupane	Step by step
Whiti te ra!	Towards sunlight!

The first Haka ever danced overseas at a rugby match was that performed by the New Zealand Native team during their 1888–9 tour of Britain. *(A number of different translations for this Haka exist – some more belligerent than others.)*

———————————— ON GOD AND DICE ————————————

God's dice always have a lucky roll.
— SOPHOCLES (497–406BC)

The devil invented dice.
— ST AUGUSTINE (AD354–430)

The dice of God are always loaded.
— RALPH WALDO EMERSON (1803–82)

God does not play dice with the Universe.
— ALBERT EINSTEIN (1879–1955), objecting to quantum theory

—— SOME SPORTING MEDICAL COMPLAINTS ——

Below are the medical translations for some colloquial sporting injuries:

Arm wrestler's arm.. radial nerve palsy[†]
Athlete's foot................ fungal disease – epidermophyton floccosum
Athlete's heel... plantar fasciitis
Athlete's groin .... adductor tendinitis
Bunions .... hallux valgus
Cauliflower ear..................... subperichondral auricular haematoma
Cheerleader's hand..................... median palmar digital neuropathy
Clergyman's throat .... chronic pharyngitis
Climber's elbow..................................... medial epicondylitis
Computer-gamer's palm........................... central palmar blister
Computer-gamer's palsy........................... distal ulnar neuropathy
Cyclist's handlebar palsy................................ ulnar neuropathy
Golfers' elbow .... medial epicondylitis
Golfer's hip .... trochanteric bursitis
Housemaid's knee .... prepatellar bursitis
Jogger's foot .... medial plantar nerve entrapment
Jogger's nipple .... friction-induced dermatitis with lichenification
Jumper's knee .... patella tendinitis
Pedal pusher's palsy.................................. sciatic neuropathy
Pitcher's elbow .... rotator cuff tendinitis
Pitcher's thumb.................................... digital nerve neuroma
Punch drunk... dementia pugilistica
Road runner's foot............................... calcaneal stress fracture
Rope skipper's thigh .... lateral femoral cutaneous neuropathy
Runner's knee........................ iliotibial band friction syndrome
Runner's stitch .... praecordial catch syndrome
Runner's toe.................................... metatarsal stress fracture
Shin splints.................................. medial tibial stress syndrome
Snowboarder's ankle........................... fracture of the lateral talus
Squash player's palsy .... tenosynovitis of the extensor pollicis longus
Swimmer's ear... otitis externa
Swimmer's goggle headache .... supraorbital neuropathy
Tennis elbow .... lateral epicondylitis
Tennis leg .... medial head of gastrocnemius rupture
Trigger finger .... stenosing tenosynovitis
Turf toe .... sprain of the first metatarsophalangeal joint
Unicyclist's groin .... sciatic neuropathy
Weightlifter's shoulder .... suprascapular neuropathy
Yoga guru's footdrop[‡].............. common peroneal nerve compression

[†] The radial nerve can also be damaged by prolonged or inappropriate use of handcuffs.
[‡] Also known as 'strawberry picker's footdrop'. · (See *Focal Dystonia, Yips, &c.* on p.26.)

———————— WODEHOUSE ON CROSSWORDS ————————

To a man who has been beating his head against the wall for twenty minutes over a single anagram, it is g. and wormwood to read that the Provost of Eton measures the time needed to boil his breakfast egg by the time needed to solve *The Times* crossword – and the Provost hates his eggs hard-boiled.

— P.G. WODEHOUSE

———————— LAS VEGAS CASINO HIERARCHY ————————

TABLE GAMES

DEALER
STICKMAN (craps)
BOXMAN
FLOORMAN
PIT BOSS
GAMES SHIFT MANAGER
CASINO MANAGER
GENERAL MANAGER

SLOT MACHINES

CHANGE GIRL
CAROUSEL ATTENDANT
FLOORMAN
ASSISTANT SHIFT MANAGER
SHIFT MANAGER
DIRECTOR OF SLOTS
GENERAL MANAGER

———————— THREE CARD MONTE ————————

Three Card Monte – otherwise known as *Find the Lady* or *Bonneteau* – is one of the oldest scams. Three cards, usually two black cards and a red Queen, are placed (by the *tosser*) on a table and shuffled before your eyes. You have to find the lady. Although to most players it seems that only the *tosser* is involved, all such scams employ *ropers* who crowd the table, *shills* who pretend to be winning punters, and *scouts* who keep a look-out for the law. Sometimes the *shills* or *ropers* will 'help' a punter by covertly turning down the corner of the Queen when the *tosser* is not looking – only for the *tosser* to sneakily straighten that card and bend the corner of another. Clearly, the only reliable way to win this game is never to play. However, if you are tempted, the best advice is this: follow the dealer's hands very closely until you are absolutely certain beyond any doubt that you have identified the Queen. Then, bet on one of the other two cards, thus increasing your chance of winning from zero to fifty per-cent. That said, if by chance you do win there is a high probability that a *scout* will raise the alarm and the game will be abandoned before you have collected your money, or that you will be pursued and 'relieved' of your winnings.

—————————— THE BENEFITS OF LACROSSE ——————————

Lacrosse requires qualities of obedience, courage, and unselfishness for the sake of the side – a player who attempts to keep the ball instead of passing it, being absolutely useless – and is full of interest on account of the various kinds of skill required, fleetness of foot, quickness of eye, strength of wrist, and a great deal of judgment and knack ... The game of lacrosse well played is a beautiful sight, the actions of the players being so full of grace and agility. The skill required, moreover, is so great that the attempt to acquire it is splendid training in courage and perseverance.

— DAME FRANCIS JANE DOVE, *c.*1890
Headmistress at St Leonard's School for Girls, St Andrews, Scotland

—————————— IDLE ROYAL AMUSEMENTS ——————————

For the birthday of the Duchess of Würtemberg in 1798, the British royal family assembled in Maiden Castle, in Dorchester, to watch these sports:

To be played for at CRICKET – *a round of Beef.*
A pound of Tobacco to be GRINNED *for.*
A barrel of Beer to be rolled down the hill: a prize to whoever STOPS *it.*
A Goose to be DIVED *for.*
A Good Hat to be CUDGELLED *for.*
Half a Guinea to the rider of the ass who wins the
best of three heats by COMING IN LAST.
A PIG *– prize to whoever catches him by the tail.*

—————————— PASCAL ON ENNUI ——————————

Nothing is as unbearable to man as to be completely at rest, without passion, without business, without diversion, without employment. This is when he feels his nothingness, his deprivation, his insufficiency, his dependency, his impotence, his hollowness. Presently, and from the depths of his soul he will bring up ennui, blackness, sadness, grief, resentment, despair.

— BLAISE PASCAL, *Pensées,* 1670

—————————— BELOW THE BELT ——————————

The boxing belt is an imaginary line from the navel to the top of the hips.

CRYPTIC CROSSWORD CODES

A few abbreviations and codes commonly used in cryptic crossword clues:

Anagram 'signposts' are often used to indicate an anagram is in the clue:
torn · scrambled · confused · wild · exploding · twisted · improved · new
shuffle(d) · shaken · reform(ed) · jumbled · drunken · unusual · badly · etc.

clue	possible interpretation
sailor	AB; jack; tar; salt; rating
flower	river
asleep; snoring; dreaming	zz
nil; duck; love; zero	o
horse	gg; nag
abstainer	tt
posh; upper class	U
bible; testaments	OT; NT
journalist	ed(itor)
spies; spooks	CIA
soldiers	GI; TA; RE; RA; etc.
painter	RA; rope
rugby	RU

clue	possible interpretation
football	FA
mother	ma; mom
ship	ss
way; road	rd, ave, st, lane
the French	le; la
of German	der; die; das
the Spanish	el
of French	de
model; car; ford	t
worker	ant; bee; drone
holy man	st
short time	min, hr, sec, tim
bloomer	flower
worker	ant

Days of the week .... ((M)on)day; ((W)ed)nesday; etc.
Months of the year .... ((J)an.)uary; ((F)eb.)ruary; etc.
Compass point (directions).... (N)orth; (S)outh; (N)orth (E)asterly; etc.
Weights and measures .... (K)ilo; (G)ram; (T)on; (lb) pound; etc.
Musical abbreviations.. ....*piano* (p) soft(ly); *forte* (f) loud(ly); etc.
Military ranks .... CO; NCO; (GEN)eral; (COL)onel; etc.
Playing cards... (Q)ueen; (J)ack; (K)nave; (K)ing; hearts; diamonds; etc.
American States .... NY; PA; CI; CA; TX; etc.
Country codes .... UK; GB; NI; USA; UN; FRA; etc.
Chemical symbols..... Gold (Au) or 'cre'; Copper (Cu); Silver (Ag); etc.

Numerals				
I 1	V 5	IX........ 9	L 50	M.... 1000
II 2	VI........ 6	X 10	LX...... 60	MD.. 1500
III....... 3	VII....... 7	XI 11	C..... 100	MM . 2000
	IV....... 4	VIII..... 8	XV 15	D 500

Some abbreviations		
eg........ for example	ie....... ...... that is	(G)PO .. . post office
PC .... policeman	nb..... .... note	is.............. island
MD; GP ...... doctor	YR .... year(ly)	r................ road
MP .... politician	RN ...... Royal Navy	o......... .. ring; hole
CE .. Church of Eng.	X..... cross; kiss; love	ng........... no good
	c....... circa; century	ac......... accountant

——————— AN ANGLER'S CALENDAR ———————

Angling may be said to be so like the mathematics,
that it can never be fully learnt.
— IZAAK WALTON, *The Compleat Angler*, 1653

This angling calendar is from an untitled German text (*c.*1493) by van
der Goes, translated in 1872 into English and Flemish by Alfred Denison:

The SALMON in April and May, and a little while after it is at its very best and the salmon remains so till the day of St James. Then it must be left to St Andrew's Day and it is best between St Michael's Mass and St Martin's.

The PIKE is best in July, only the pike is good at all times, only excepted when he sees the rye he spawns.

The forepart of a PIKE or CARP is better always than the hind part, it is the same with other fishes.

A TENCH is always best in June.

The PERCH is always good except in May or April.

The BREAM and MACKEREL are good in February and March.

The MULLET is good in March or April.

A KULLUNCK is best at Candlemas Day and continues good in April.

The RUDD is good in February and March and falls off in May.

The GUDGEONS are good in February, March, and April, till May. Only the young Gudgeon is always good with parsley.

A BLEAK is best in Autumn.

The STICKLEBACKS are good in March, and in the beginning of May, when they are full they shall be stirred with eggs.

The EEL is good in May till the day of the Assumption of Our Lady.

A LAMPREY is never better than in May.

A LAMPHERN, the brother of the lamprey, is good from the thirteenth Mass to the day of Our Lady's Annunciation.

The CRAYFISH is best in March and April and particularly when the moon increases, then they are so much the better.

Fly-fishing may be a very pleasant amusement;
but angling or float-fishing I can only compare to a stick and a string,
with a worm at one end and a fool at the other.
— SAMUEL JOHNSON [attrib.]

HOUDINI'S CODE

Harry Houdini created an elaborate code with his wife-cum-glamorous-assistant Bess to perform 'mind reading' illusions involving numbers. Bess would indicate, say, the serial number of a dollar bill, or a punter's date of birth, by constructing a sentence utilizing the following code words:

1 . . . . pray | 3 . . . . say | 5 . . . . tell | 7 . . . . . speak | 9 . . . . look
2 . . . . answer | 4. . . . . now | 6 . . . . please | 8. . . quickly | 0 . . be quick

For example the drivers license number 4785932 would be revealed by:

Now! Speak to me, oh great Houdini! Quickly tell me!
Look deep within your mind, and say the answer!

DRINKING GAME ADMINISTRATION

It is outside the scope of this *Miscellany* to detail the many and various drinking games which exist (e.g. *ibble-dibble*, *bunnies*, or *drink while you think*). However, a few organizational and administrative customs and traditions seem to be common to most drinking games around the world:

MR CHAIRMAN · In sole charge of setting and enforcing all rules and fines. All conversations must go 'through' the Chairman. When the Chairman drinks, everyone drinks.

MR WEIGHTS & MEASURES · In charge of ensuring that all have adequate drinks, and that any fines levied are completely consumed. He is particularly concerned with short measures and 'spillage'.

MR CHIEF SNEAK · Reports any rule-breaking to the Chairman.

THUMB MASTER · If at any time the Thumb Master places his thumb on the edge of the table, every other player must follow suit. The last player to notice and place his thumb is fined.

POINTING is forbidden. Only elbows may be used to indicate. Only LEFT-HANDED DRINKING is usually permitted. Some play the rule known as HALF HOUR HAND when the drinking hand changes every thirty minutes. FIRST NAMES are replaced by surnames or nicknames. SWEARING is forbidden. Drinks that are placed perilously close to the edge of a table (say a finger's length) may be deemed by the CHIEF SNEAK to be DANGEROUS PINTS – and must be imbibed forthwith. Certain words are prohibited and must be replaced by synonyms: drinks are TIPPLES or BEVERAGES, and drinking is IMBIBING; the bar is the SALOON; fingers are DIGITS; etc. If a COIN is dropped into a glass, its contents must be finished.

--------------- ON IDLENESS & IDLERS ---------------

SAMUEL JOHNSON · If you are idle, be not solitary; if you are solitary, be not idle.

HENRY FORD · There is no place in civilization for the idler. None of us has any right to ease.

ST MATTHEW · Every idle word that men shall speak, they shall give account thereof in the day of judgment.

OSCAR WILDE · The condition of perfection is idleness.

THOMAS PYNCHON · Writers of course are the mavens of sloth ... Idle dreaming is often the essence of what we do.

SOMERSET MAUGHAM · It was such a lovely day. I thought it was a pity to get up.

LORD CRANBORNE · [on Kenneth Clark MP] One of the reasons he would be good is that he is idle. There is a lot to be said for idle leaders.

GEORGE ELIOT · There's many a one who would be idle if hunger didn't pinch him; but the stomach sets us to work.

OSCAR WILDE · I feel an irresistible desire to wander, and go to Japan, where I will pass my youth, sitting under an almond tree, drinking amber tea out of a blue cup, and looking at a landscape without perspective.

THOMAS À KEMPIS · *Numquam sis ex toto otiosus, sed aut legens, aut scribens, aut orans, aut meditans, aut aliquid utilitatis pro communi laborans.* [Never be completely idle, but either reading, or writing, or praying, or meditating, or at some useful work for the common good.]

SAMUEL JOHNSON · We would all be idle if we could.

JEAN JACQUES ROUSSEAU · I love to busy myself about trifles, to begin a hundred things and not finish one of them ... in short to fritter the whole day away inconsequentially ... and to follow nothing but the whim of the moment.

SPANISH PROVERB · How perfect it is to do nothing, and then afterwards rest.

JEROME K. JEROME · There are plenty of lazy people and plenty of slowcoaches, but a genuine idler is a rarity.

LORENZO DI COMO · An idle life is a prize to be labored for; to be idle is the quintessence of life.

D.E. McCONNELL · Perhaps the greatest cause of misery and wretchedness in social life is idleness. The want of something to do is what makes people wicked and miserable. It breeds selfishness, mischief-making, envy, jealousy and vice, in all its most dreadful forms.

──────────── ON IDLENESS & IDLERS cont. ────────────

JAMES THURBER · It is better to have loafed and lost than never to have loafed at all.

W.F. HARGREAVES ·
    I'm Burlington Bertie,
    I rise at ten-thirty
    And saunter along like a toff.
    I walk down the Strand
    With my gloves on my hand,
    Then I walk down again
        with them off.
(See also Burlington Bertie on p.40.)

LORD CHESTERFIELD · Idleness is only the refuge of weak minds. (See also p.92.)

ISAAC WATTS · Tis the voice of the sluggard, I heard him complain 'You have waked me too soon, I must slumber again.'

SAMUEL JOHNSON · I have, all my life long, been lying till noon; yet I tell all young men, and tell them with all great sincerity, that nobody who does not rise early will ever do any good.

F SCOTT FITZGERALD ·
Sometimes I think that idlers seem to be a special class for whom nothing can be planned, plead as one will with them …

CHINESE PROVERB · It has ever been thus, that young idlers make old penitents.

JEROME K. JEROME · I like work; it fascinates me. I can sit and look at it for hours. I love to keep it by me; the idea of getting rid of it nearly breaks my heart.

──────────── SOME ENDURANCE RACES ────────────

Race	*description of the madness*
Marathon des Sables[†]	151-mile race run over 6 days in the Sahara
Everest Marathon	marathon at an altitude of 5,184m
South-Pole Ultramarathon	45km race in snow shoes to the South Pole
Badwater	135 miles from Death Valley to Mount Whitney
Cornbelt Run	run continuously for 24 hours round a 400m track
JFK Ultra	50 miles with over 800 competitors
Comrades Marathon	Durban to Pietermaritzburg, 89km
Devil o' the Highlands	43 miles up and down Scottish mountains
Jungle Run	200km over 7 days through the Amazon jungle
Self-transcendence Race	longest foot race in the world, 3,100 miles
Spartathlon	historical race, run from Athens to Sparta, 246km
Escarpment Trail	30km mountain race over the Catskill mountains
Gobi March	7-day, 155-mile race across the Gobi desert

† During this marathon a camel ensures that only those able to keep up can continue. The camel plods along behind the race, and any runner passed by the beast is disqualified.

———————— SI's SPORTSMAN OF THE YEAR ————————

The roll-call of those awarded *Sports Illustrated*'s Sportsman of the Year:

'54 . . . . Roger Bannister, *track*
'55 . . . . Johnny Podres, *baseball*
'56 . . . . . Bobby Joe Morrow, *track*
'57 . . . . Stan Musial, *baseball*
'58 . . . . Rafer Johnson, *track*
'59 . . . . Ingemar Johansson, *boxing*
'60 . . . . Arnold Palmer, *golf*
'61 . . . . Jerry Lucas, *basketball*
'62 . . . . Terry Baker, *football*
'63 . . . . Pete Rozelle, *football*
'64 . . . . Ken Venturi, *golf*
'65 . . . . Sandy Koufax, *baseball*
'66 . . . . Jim Ryun, *track*
'67 . . . . . Carl Yastrzemski, *baseball*
'68 . . . . Bill Russell, *basketball*
'69 . . . . Tom Seaver, *baseball*
'70 . . . . Bobby Orr, *hockey*
'71 . . . . Lee Trevino, *golf*
'72 . . . . Billie Jean King, *tennis*
          John Wooden, *basketball*
'73 . . . . . Jackie Stewart, *auto racing*
'74 . . . . Muhammad Ali, *boxing*
'75 . . . . Pete Rose, *baseball*
'76 . . . . Chris Evert, *tennis*
'77 . . . . Steve Cauthen, *horse racing*
'78 . . . . Jack Nicklaus, *golf*
'79 . . . . Terry Bradshaw, *football*
          Willie Stargell, *baseball*
'80 . . . . US Olympic Hockey Team
'81 . . . . Sugar Ray Leonard, *boxing*
'82 . . . . Wayne Gretzky, *hockey*
'83 . . . . Mary Decker, *track*
'84 . . . . Edwin Moses, *track*
          Mary Lou Retton, *gymnastics*

'85 . . . . Kareem Abdul-Jabbar
          basketball
'86 . . . . Joe Paterno, *football*
'87 . . . . *8 Athletes Who Care*
          Bob Bourne, *hockey*
          Kip Keino, *track*
          Judi Brown King, *track*
          Dale Murphy, *baseball*
          Chip Rives, *football*
          Patty Sheehan, *golf*
          Rory Sparrow, *basketball*
          Reggie Williams, *football*
'88 . . . . Orel Hershiser, *baseball*
'89 . . . . Greg LeMond, *cycling*
'90 . . . . Joe Montana, *football*
'91 . . . . Michael Jordan, *basketball*
'92 . . . . Arthur Ashe, *tennis*
'93 . . . . Don Shula, *football*
'94 . . . . . Bonnie Blair, *speed skating*
          Johan Olav Koss, *speed skating*
'95 . . . . Cal Ripken Jr., *baseball*
'96 . . . . Tiger Woods, *golf*
'97 . . . . Dean Smith, *basketball*
'98 . . . . . . Mark McGwire, *baseball*
          Sammy Sosa, *baseball*
'99 . . . . . U.S. Women's World Cup
          Soccer Team
'00 . . . . Tiger Woods, *golf*
'01 . . . . . . Randy Johnson, *baseball*
          Curt Schilling, *baseball*
'02 . . . . . . Lance Armstrong, *cycling*
'03 . . . . Tim Duncan, *basketball*
          David Robinson, *basketball*
'04 . . . . Boston Red Sox

———————— CRICKETING DISMISSALS ————————

Hit Wicket · Caught · Bowled · Run Out · Handled Ball · Stumped
Hit Ball Twice · Timed Out[†] · Leg Before Wicket · Obstructed Field
† *New batsmen are allowed 3 minutes to get to their crease after the fall of a wicket.*

—— SOME PREFERRED COARSE FISHING BAITS ——

Bait	*Type of fish*		
Hempseed	Roach	Bread paste	Barbel & tench
Dog-biscuits	Carp & chub	Lob worms	Perch
Sweetcorn	Carp, barbel, & tench	Marshmallows	Carp
Spam	Chub, barbel, & carp	Casters‡	Dace, roach, & chub
Cheese	Chub	Maggots	Most fish
Boilies†	Carp	Slugs	Chub
		Cat food	Carp

† Balls of paste mixed with egg and boiled into hard pellets, so small fish cannot nibble.
‡ Chrysalis stage of maggots. · [Clearly such a table can only hope to annoy fishermen.]

—— TYPOLOGY OF COMPETITIVE BOOMERANG ——

Across the world, notably in Australia and America, boomerangs are thrown competitively in a number of different events, some of which are:

ACCURACY · throws are made from the center of a set of circles marked on the ground. Points are awarded for how close it lands to the bullseye.

TRICK CATCH · for example, one-handed, behind the back, under the leg, caught with feet, and so on. (Tricks are also performed with two boomerangs simultaneously.)

AUSTRALIAN ROUND · tests the distance of the throw, the accuracy of the return, and the skill of the catch over five attempts.

FAST CATCH · making five throws and catches as quickly as possible with the same boomerang.

ENDURANCE · involves making as many throws as possible over a five-minute period.

DOUBLES · throwing and catching two boomerangs at the same time.

MAXIMUM TIME ALOFT [MTA] · the longest of five throws to stay in the air – the current record is 17 minutes 6 seconds by John Gorski, in Ohio on 8 August 1993.

JUGGLING · keeping two or more boomerangs in the air at the same time for as long as possible.

LONG DISTANCE · where points are awarded on distance thrown.

FREESTYLE · where points are awarded for height, speed, style, and general finesse.

Many of these events are played as team events, usually with four members per team. One team event involves three players playing FAST CATCH for the time that the fourth plays MTA.

[Most standard boomerang events require each boomerang to fly a minimum of 20 meters out from the throw to be counted.]

CABER TOSSING

Tossing the caber is a key element of any Highland Games. The caber itself is a tree trunk (denuded of its branches) of unspecified size – though it has to be of a length and weight to challenge even the strongest athlete. (Occasionally, cabers are submerged overnight in nearby lochs to increase their weight.) Athletes are presented with the caber in its vertical position, and their challenge is to upend the trunk in a perfect longitudinal revolution, so that the caber's top faces them. A perfect toss should land directly in front of the tosser, at '12 o'clock', without deviating to the right or left. Tossers are given three attempts with a caber – of which the best throw is scored. If a new caber cannot be tossed it may be progressively shortened until an athlete is successful, after which the caber may never be modified. Perhaps the most famous challenge is presented by the Braemar Caber which weighs 54·5kg (120lb) and is 5·79m (19ft) long. It was first successfully tossed by 51-year-old George Clark in 1951.

JOIN-THE-DOT PUZZLES

The 16 circles can be joined with 6 straight lines; the 9 squares can be joined with 4 straight lines. (In both cases the lines must be continuous.)
For solutions, turn to p.160.

THE FIFTEEN POINTS OF A GOOD HORSE

Wynkyn de Worde (d.1535) was an Alsatian-born pioneer of printing. He was employed at William Caxton's London press, and took control of the business when Caxton died in 1491. De Worde was the first printer in England to employ italic typefaces. In one of the many publications he printed de Worde enumerated the fifteen points required of a good horse:

A good horse sholde have three propyrtees of a man, three of a woman, three of a foxe, three of a haare, and three of an asse.

Of a MAN. Bolde, prowde, and hardye.
Of a WOMAN. Fayre-breasted, faire of heere, and easy to move.
Of a FOXE. A fair taylle, short eers, with a good trotte.
Of a HAARE. A grate eye, a dry head, and well rennynge.
Of an ASSE. A bygge chynn, a flat legge, and a good hoof.

———— SOME GAMBLING TERMINOLOGY ————

Action..... the amount of money in a pot; a high-rolling gambling table
Anchor man......... the player, to the right of the dealer, who plays last
Ante...................... a sum paid into the pot before the game starts
Bad beat .... snatching defeat from the jaws of victory
Beard.......... a runner for a gambler who wants to remain anonymous
Bet the pot .... to bet a sum equal to that in the pot
Bones................................. colloquialism for dice or dominoes
Bottom deal.............. a (crooked) deal from the bottom of the deck
Burned cards .... cards discarded from a pack before dealing
Call .... in poker, to match the last bet
Carte blanche........................... a hand of cards with no face-card
Chalk .... a favorite
Churn............... betting with money you have won (until you lose)
Cold (*or* stacked) deck .... a pre-ordered rigged pack of cards
Comp .... 'free' incentives given by the House to high rollers[†]
Court card.. .... King, Queen, Jack
Doublet....................... a domino with the same value at each end
Edge .... the statistical advantage the House enjoys in each game
Faites vos jeux ....Place your bets
Fishing .. .. remaining in a card game in the hope of a vital card
Frenchies............. ostensibly honest players who will cheat if need be
Hold your own ....break even
Juice .... the profit made by the House
Lines..odds
Parlay.........a bet which depends on a series of propositions occurring
Press................................. ......to increase one's original stake
Pressing.. ....adding money just won to the next bet
Rien ne va plus...................... ... .No more bets
Runt................................. a poker hand worth less than a pair
Rush........... .... a winning streak
Soft hand ....a blackjack hand where an Ace is counted as 11
Steal...................... to win a game by bluffing; or, simply, to steal
Stock..................................... ....the undealt cards
Talon .... the pile of discarded cards
Toke................................... .... to tip the dealer
Trey.......... ....a 3 of any suit in cards
Underlay...... ....a bad or 'unlucky' bet
Vig (*or* vigorish)............. the percentage of any House or bookmaker
Welsh (welch)........................ ... .to fail to repay a debt
Yarborough.... .....a whist or bridge hand with no card higher than a 9

† A classic American *comp* term popular in Las Vegas is 'RFB', which stands for Room,
Food & Beverages. · (See also Slang, p.22; Dice Odds, p.106; and Rigged Dice, p.116.)

TWO DICE ODDS

no.	ways		probability	odds
12	1	*(box cars)*	0·0278	35/1
11	2		0·0556	17/1
10	3		0·0833	11/1
9	4		0·1111	8/1
8	5		0·1389	31/5
7	6		0·1667	5/1
6	5		0·1389	31/5
5	4		0·1111	8/1
4	3		0·0833	11/1
3	2		0·0556	17/1
2	1	*(snake eyes)*	0·0278	35/1

A score achieved by rolling 2 identical dice (e.g. a total of 6 with 3/3 rather than 4/2 or 5/1) is considered to have been made the 'hard way'. Here, the odds expressed are those that would be given by a bookmaker: 35/1 = 1 in 36.

SPORT & MONEY

'A gentleman never competes for money, directly or indirectly. Make no mistake about this. No matter how winding the road may be that eventually brings to sovereign into the pocket, it is the price of what should be dearer to you than anything else: your honor.'

WALTER CAMP, 1893
the 'Father of American Football'

'If they spent a $1m a year living, that's a great lifestyle. If half went to taxes and fees and whatnot, and they spent 10%, 40%'s left. A guy saves $40m of $100m and he bought tax-free bonds and he got 5%. So, he's got $2m a year coming in forever…'

CURTIS POLK, 1997
sports' agent, on his clients

JANE AUSTEN ON BASEBALL vs BOOKS

… it was not very wonderful that Catherine, who had by nature nothing heroic about her, should prefer cricket, baseball, riding on horseback, and running about the country at the age of fourteen, to books – or at least books of information – for, provided that nothing like useful knowledge could be gained from them, provided they were all story and no reflection, she had never any objection to books at all.

— JANE AUSTEN, *Northanger Abbey*, 1818

─────── SWIMMING THE ENGLISH CHANNEL ───────

The first successful cross-Channel swim was accomplished by Captain Matthew Webb, who, heavily greased with porpoise oil, took 21¾ hours to swim from Dover to Calais on 24–5 August 1875. (Only twelve days earlier, Webb had been forced by poor weather to abandon an attempt at the crossing, complaining that there was 'too much sea on'.) Webb swam a slow and stately breast-stroke (20 to the minute), and fortified himself with beef-tea, beer, coffee, cod-liver oil, and – to counteract the effects of a nasty sting by a yellow star-fish – even brandy. Webb's route was thus:

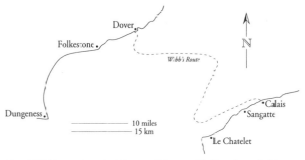

After Webb's crossing the Mayor of Dover said, 'I make so bold to say that I don't believe that in the future history of the world any such feat will be performed by anybody else'. But, while it took 36 years for Webb's feat to be repeated, since then a multitude have made the crossing, employing a range of styles: backstroke, Australian crawl, and the curious Trudgeon stroke (scissor kicks with a double over-arm). Below are a few records:

date	feat (CROSSING DIRECTION)	name	time
1875	*1st solo crossing* (E–F)	M. Webb [UK]	21:45
1911	*2nd solo crossing* (E–F)	T.W. Burgess [UK]	22:35
1923	*1st solo crossing* (F–E)	Enrico Tiraboschi [ITA]	16:33
1926	*1st female solo crossing* (F–E)	Gertrude Ederle [USA]	14:39
1934	*1st to beat Webb's time* (E–F)	E. Temme [UK]	15:34
1951	*1st female solo crossing* (E–F)	Florence Chadwick [USA]	16:19
1961	*1st non-stop return crossing*	Antonio Abertondo [ARG]	43:10
1978	*1st under-16* [13y 233d] (E–F)	Karl Beniston [UK]	12:25
1981	*1st triple crossing* (E–F–E–F)	Jon Erikson [USA]	38:27
1982	*1st crossing by a Chilean* (E–F)	Victor Contraras [CHI]	12:02
1989	*1st butterfly-stroke* (E–F)	Vicki Keith [CAN]	23:33

Glaswegian Jabez Wolffe attempted the Channel crossing 22 times and failed on each occasion. In 1911 a bagpipe player accompanied him by boat to help him set a rhythm – but to no avail. For the curious, tragic, and strangely ironic drowning of Captain Matthew Webb see p.42.

HAT-TRICKS

In sporting terms, the hat-trick was originally a cricketing phrase for the feat of taking three wickets in three successive balls. There is some debate as to the origin of the term – some claiming that the bowler was given a new hat by the members of his team[†]; others claiming that the bowler's hat was used as the receptacle for an informal whip-round. Either way, since the C19th the term has escaped the boundaries of the cricket pitch, and is generally used for any kind of triplet in any sporting endeavor.

† In 1858 D.V.P. Wright actually was presented with a new hat having bowled a hat-trick.

FOLDING 'THE BANDIT'

HOT BATHS, BATHING, & EUREKA!

Few things are more conducive to idleness than a hot bath and – Archimedes aside[†] – the bathtub can rightly be viewed as offering some respite from the exertions of everyday life. It is no mistake that victorious gladiators would repair to the baths of imperial Rome, or that sports physios sometimes recommend hot baths for post-match warm-downs. The following classification of bathing-water temperatures is from the 1904 edition of B. Bradshaw's *Bathing Places and Climatic Health Resorts*:

Cold	40–50°F	Warm	90
Cool	60	Hot	100–103
Tepid	70–80	Hot as can be borne	115–125

'Hot baths, if continued for any length of time, are very enervating and should usually be followed by a cool sponging of the surface.'

† Syracusan mathematician Archimedes (*c.*287–212BC) was commissioned by King Hiero II to test the purity of a gold votive crown which the King suspected had been forged with inferior metals. Archimedes, observing while getting into his bath that some of the bathwater overflowed, quickly realized that an object floating in a liquid displaces a weight of liquid equal to its own weight. Since silver is less dense than gold, 1lb of silver is bulkier than a 1lb of gold and will displace more water. Thus Archimedes was able to prove that Hiero's crown was impure. This observation was famously accompanied by the exclamation *Eureka!* – the Greek for 'I have found it!'.

—— FRANKLIN'S ANTI-IDLING TIMETABLE ——

Benjamin Franklin (1706–90) was a sworn enemy of idling and the idle. 'Trouble springs from idleness, and grievous toil from needless ease,' he wrote, asserting that 'sloth, like rust, consumes faster than labor wears, while the used key is always bright'. In a characteristically logical attempt to maximize the use of his own time, Franklin carried with him a small book in which he tabulated a 'scheme of employment' for a natural day:

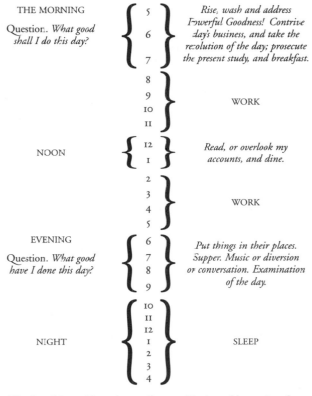

THE MORNING Question. *What good shall I do this day?*	{ 5 6 7 }	*Rise, wash and address Powerful Goodness! Contrive day's business, and take the resolution of the day; prosecute the present study, and breakfast.*
	8 9 10 11 }	WORK
NOON	{ 12 1 }	*Read, or overlook my accounts, and dine.*
	2 3 4 5 }	WORK
EVENING Question. *What good have I done this day?*	{ 6 7 8 9 }	*Put things in their places. Supper. Music or diversion or conversation. Examination of the day.*
NIGHT	{ 10 11 12 1 2 3 4 }	SLEEP

Franklin found it problematic to adhere to his timetable, noting that a man who must interact with others cannot structure his time like one who works alone. Although he concluded 'tho' I never arrived at the perfection I had been so ambitious of obtaining ... I was, by the endeavor, a better and a happier man than I otherwise should have been'.

——————————— THE LANGUAGE OF SPORT ———————————

Some sporting words and phrases in day-to-day currency, or of curiosity:

STICKY WICKET · a cricketing term for grass which is drying after having been soaked by rain. Such a wicket favors spin bowlers who can use the surface to make the ball turn dramatically.

RAIN CHECK · the portion of a ticket which, in the event of rain, would secure free entrance into another game.

BATTLE ROYAL · an outlawed type of boxing where 3 or more men would fight together in a ring; the winner was the last man standing. (Also a cockfighting term.)

GREEN FLY · a sporting 'groupie' who craves the attention of professional (baseball) athletes. In Britain, the expression BLUE TACK is used to describe girls who flock to Oxford and Cambridge 'blues' athletes. (Aka: BASEBALL ANNIE.)

BLACKGUARD · a foul in fives when a serve hits the front wall without having hit the side wall first. Also a general term for a ruffian, hoodlum, or ne'erdowell.

PEG OUT · croquet term for when a ball has been played through all of the hoops and is hit on the central peg to complete its circuit.

WALKING IN · in cricket, when fielders stroll into their positions as the bowler runs in so that they are moving when the ball is played.

TIGHT LINES · encouragement of good luck given by one fisherman to another.

HOT STOVE LEAGUE · describes the fans who banter about their sports during the off-season. Similar to MONDAY MORNING QUARTERBACKS who debate the failings of their team on the previous Saturday.

KIGGLE-KAGGLE · describes the rocking of a curling stone that has not been thrown squarely.

SOUTHPAW · a lefthander, usually associated with baseball pitchers and boxers. It has been suggested that to avoid the glare of the sun, baseball diamonds were built with home plate facing west, and thus the throwing arm of lefthanded pitchers would usually be south. Southpaw boxers are those that lead with the right hand and foot.

INTESTINAL FORTITUDE · guts.

HOSPITAL PASS · when a ball is badly passed to a team-mate so that they are drawn into danger.

SUDDEN DEATH · any scoring system whereby the next to win a point wins the match.

NIGHT WATCHMAN · in cricket, a batsman whose job it is to play safe at the end of the day, and carry his innings over to the next morning.

SITZMARK · the splendid German term for a depression left in the snow by a fallen skier.

THE WALL · psychological barrier confronting endurance athletes.

DUKES · slang for fists (as in 'put up your dukes'), possibly deriving from the Cockney rhyming slang: Duke of York = fork = fingers on the hand.

(GUARDIAN) ANGEL · a cloud that shields from the sun the eyes of a fielder about to make a catch

SHARK · one who under-represents their sporting abilities to win money in a competitive game. (Also a HUSTLER or BANDIT).

BISQUE · an (often informal) 'free' stroke given to weaker players in sports such as croquet, tennis, and golf (see Mulligan on p.27).

FUNGO · a warm-up or practice shot, not counted in a game.

ANCHOR · the last man on a tug-of-war rope; the last player in a number of team sports; or the final participant of a relay team.

SCHUSSBOOMER · one who skies recklessly or without control.

DEKE [short for DECOY] · to fake a movement in one direction before moving in another to deceive an opponent (also DUMMY, or THE WOMBA).

SLEDGING · the dubious 'art' of barracking a batsmen in cricket; perfected by Australian fielders.

BRONX CHEER · a raspberry.

ARTIST or PAINTER· a weak boxer who is always 'on the canvas'.

ENGLISH · imparting spin on a ball, usually in billiards or snooker. BODY ENGLISH is the futile but instinctive attempt to influence the trajectory of a ball already in motion by contorting one's body in the direction one wants it to go.

THE NINETEENTH (HOLE) · the golf clubhouse bar.

CAPPED · to have played for one's national side in a sport.

DIVE · to fake or exaggerate an injury to waste time, or to get an opponent penalized.

GHOST · to maintain a low profile during a team game in the hope or remaining unmarked.

DAISY CUTTER · any ball that rolls along or just above the ground.

(UN)FORCED ERROR · errors made either by the good play of an opponent, or simply by a mistake of the player.

GARRISON FINISH · to come from behind and affect a spectacular win; after the jockey Edward 'Snapper' Garrison.

MONOPOLY MONEY

At the beginning of every game of Monopoly each player receives $1,500 from the Bank in the following denominations:

$2 \times \$500 \cdot 2 \times \$100 \cdot 2 \times \$50 \cdot 6 \times \$20 \cdot 5 \times \$10 \cdot 5 \times \$5 \cdot 5 \times \$1$

DISCONTINUED & DEMONSTRATION OLYMPIC SPORTS

A number of sports have been included at Olympic Games of the past as demonstration sports not eligible for medals – a practice which has been discontinued since 1992. In addition, a number of sports have fallen out of favor and are no longer part of the modern Olympic roll-call. The list below tabulates these sports, along with the last year of their inclusion:

DEMONSTRATION SPORTS		DISCONTINUED SPORTS	
American football	1932	Cricket	1900
Australian rules football	1956	Croquet‡	1900
Bandy	1952	Golf	1904
Bicycle polo†	1908	Jeu de paume	1908
Budo	1964	Lacrosse	1908
Dog sled racing	1932	Motor boating	1908
Gliding	1936	Polo	1936
Jeu de paume	1928	Racquets	1908
Korfball	1928	Roque	1904
Lacrosse	1948	Rugby union	1924
Military patrol	1948	Tug of war	1920
Pelota basque	1992		
Roller hockey	1992	
Speed skiing	1992	
Water skiing	1972	
Winter pentathlon	1948	

† *The one and only Olympic bicycle polo match was played between Germany and the Irish Bicycle Polo Association.*

‡ *All contestants in the event were French.*

Only 5 sports have been contested at every modern Olympics since 1896:

ATHLETICS · CYCLING · FENCING · GYMNASTICS · SWIMMING

For the IOC to recognize a sport (though this does not guarantee it will be contested at a Games) it must meet the following minimum criteria:

Men's sport .... *widely played in at least 75 countries on 4 continents*
Women's sport .... *widely played in at least 40 countries on 3 continents*
Winter sport .... *widely played in at least 25 countries on 3 continents*

SOLVING MARBLE SOLITAIRE

Listed here are the moves required to solve a standard thirty-two-piece game of marble solitaire – should all else have failed.

Move	*to*	*take*
d2 ⇒	d4 ∴	d3
f3 ⇒	d3 ∴	e3
e1 ⇒	e3 ∴	e2
e4 ⇒	e2 ∴	e3
c1 ⇒	e1 ∴	d1
e1 ⇒	e3 ∴	e2
e6 ⇒	e4 ∴	e5
g5 ⇒	e5 ∴	f5
d5 ⇒	f5 ∴	e5
g3 ⇒	g5 ∴	g4
g5 ⇒	e5 ∴	f5
b5 ⇒	d5 ∴	c5
c7 ⇒	c5 ∴	c6
c4 ⇒	c6 ∴	c5
e7 ⇒	c7 ∴	d7

Move	*to*	*take*
c7 ⇒	c5 ∴	c6
c2 ⇒	c4 ∴	c3
a3 ⇒	c3 ∴	b3
d3 ⇒	b3 ∴	c3
a5 ⇒	a3 ∴	a4
a3 ⇒	c3 ∴	b3
d5 ⇒	d3 ∴	d4
d3 ⇒	b3 ∴	c3
b3 ⇒	b5 ∴	b4
b5 ⇒	d5 ∴	c5
d5 ⇒	f5 ∴	e5
f4 ⇒	d4 ∴	e4
c4 ⇒	e4 ∴	d4
e3 ⇒	e5 ∴	e4
f5 ⇒	d5 ∴	e5
d6 ⇒	d4 ∴	d5

Solitaire is, as its name implies, a game for a solitary player; and it has the great merit that it can be played with equal enjoyment and profit by children, by invalids, and – in their spare moments – by Professors of Higher Mathematics.

— EDMOND HOYLE (1672–1769)

LOTUS-EATERS

The lotus-eaters of Greek myth dwelt on the ever-shifting sandbanks of waters near Carthage. There they ate the fruit of the lotus – not the water-lilies of Egypt, but plants with roots in the underworld that drew water from the river Lethe. This water had the power to remove all memories, and the lotus-eaters (or Lotophagi) lived in an idle, paralyzed, trancelike state with neither recollection of the past nor concept of the future, and with no desire to return to their native lands. As Odysseus sailed home from Troy, he landed on one of these sandbanks and sent three men out to explore. The men discovered the Lotophagi, ate of their fruit, and were sucked into a twilight state of idle paralysis before being dragged weeping back to their ship, pleading to be left behind. In his 1833 poem *Song of the Lotos-Eaters*, Alfred Tennyson used this myth to explore our desire to reject the prosaic world of toil for a more languorous state of idleness:

Let us swear an oath, and keep it with an equal mind,
In the hollow Lotos-land to live and lie reclined
On the hills like Gods together, careless of mankind.

————— NAVEL GAZING —————

The navel, umbilicus, omphalodium, or belly-button is the round cicatrix (scar-tissue) protuberance located on the abdomen where the umbilical cord was originally attached. Since the dawn of time the navel has been the focus of a reflective form of philosophical contemplation known as Omphalopsychism. This might be because the navel literally represents the location of birth, or perhaps because it is where the eye lazily falls when one is reclining naked. A number of Omphalopsychite groups have existed through history – perhaps the most famous of which were the Hesychasts, a sect of quietists who (from *c.*AD1050) practised gazing at the navel to induce a hypnotic reverie. The Hesychasts believed that through a rigorous regime of asceticism, devotion, and deep contemplation of the body, a mystic light – no less than the uncreated divine light of God – could be seen. The question of whether Adam and Eve had navels (given that they were created by God) is one which has vexed theologians for some time. Incidentally, a number of artists, not least Albrecht Dürer and William Blake, have chosen to depict Adam and Eve *with* omphalodia.

————— HORSE-RACING WINNING MARGINS —————

The following schematic shows the order of winning margins in racing:

```
————————————————————————————————————— nose
————————————————————————————————— short head
——————————————————————————————— head
————————————————————————— neck
———————————————————— half a length
———————————————— length
—— distance
```

A *length* is the distance from a horse's nose to the start of its tail (roughly 8 feet). In professional racing, margins tend to be measured in time: in flat racing, 1 second = 5 *lengths*; in jump racing, 1 second = 4 *lengths*. A *distance* is usually employed to describe a margin longer than 30 *lengths*.

————— PARDONING BULLS —————

In bullfighting an *indulto* is a pardon granted to a bull by the *presidente* of the fight for demonstrating extraordinary braveness. Some of the *toros célebres* (famous bulls) granted the *indulto* include: Algareño, Civilón, Gordito (who killed 21 horses during a fight in 1869), and Jaquéton – whose name is given as a nickname to other bulls considered to be brave.

——————————— PAC-MAN ———————————

The name *Pac-Man* derives from the Japanese 'paku paku' – a term that refers to the motion of the mouth as it opens and closes while eating. (The original game was called *Pukman*, though this was swiftly changed for the Western market when it became clear how easily the initial letter could be modified for obscene effect.) The game's principal designer, Toru Iwatani, claims that *Pac-Man's* iconic character was inspired when he saw a pan of pizza with a slice removed, and the marriage of maze-based game with cartoon-like food consumption developed from there. To complete a level, *Pac-Man* must gobble up the 240 *dots* and 4 *energizers* which fill each maze while being pursued by 4 *ghosts* who will eliminate one of his three lives each time they run into him. *Pac-Man* scores bonus points by eating the *fruits* and *prizes* which occasionally appear, and by eating the *ghosts* when they have been rendered temporarily vulnerable (and blue) by the *energizers*. The *ghosts* are known by a variety of names and nicknames:

Japanese name	Japanese nickname		English name	English nickname
Oikake	*Akabei*	RED	Shadow	*Blinky*
Machibuse	*Pinky*	PINK	Speedy	*Pinky*
Kimagure	*Aosuke*	CYAN	Bashful	*Inky*
Otoboke	*Guzuta*	ORANGE	Pokey	*Clyde*

Each ghost has a distinct personality: *Pinky* is nifty, often hovering just in front of *Pac-Man's* gobbling mouth; *Blinky* tends to follow in dogged pursuit; *Inky* is bashful, sometimes even fleeing from *Pac-Man*; and *Clyde* is just plain slow. Complex algorithms allow the ghosts to team up in group attacks and then disperse – an attempt by the programmers to prevent players from becoming discouraged. The Holy Grail of 'classic' *Pac-Man* (which spawned a wealth of spin-off games) is to eat every *dot*, every *energizer*, every blue *ghost*, and every *fruit* and *prize* on all 256 levels without losing a single life[†]. On 3 July 1999, Billy Mitchell became the first to accomplish this feat, playing for six hours on a single quarter.

[†] Everything *Pac-Man* gobbles has a point value: *dots* = 10 points; *energizers* = 50 points; *dark blue ghosts* = 200, 400, 800, and 1600 respectively; *cherries* = 100; *strawberries* = 300; *peaches* = 500; *apples* = 700; *grapes* = 1000; *Galaxians* = 2000; *bells* = 3000; *keys* = 5000. Billy Mitchell's maximum *Pac-Man* score therefore was an astonishing 3,333,360 points.

——— MOTTO OF THE ROYAL LIFE SAVING SOCIETY———

QUEMCUNQUE MISERUM VIDERIS HOMINEM SCIAS
whosoever you see in distress, recognize in him a fellow man

—————— RIGGED DICE ——————

For as long as dice have been used for gaming and gambling they have been fixed *(gaffed)* by dice-cheats *(mittmen)* in a variety of novel ways. *Loaded dice* are those secretly weighted – often with a substance (like mercury) that could be tapped into different places to favor a particular number – hence their nicknames of *tappers* and *peeties*. A *dead deuce* die is loaded on the 5 so that the 2 rolls more frequently. *Floated dice* work on the same principle but with

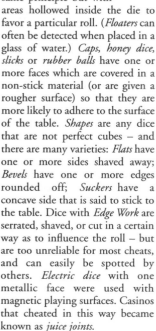

an honest layout

areas hollowed inside the die to favor a particular roll. (*Floaters* can often be detected when placed in a glass of water.) *Caps*, *honey dice*, *slicks* or *rubber balls* have one or more faces which are covered in a non-stick material (or are given a rougher surface) so that they are more likely to adhere to the surface of the table. *Shapes* are any dice that are not perfect cubes – and there are many varieties: *Flats* have one or more sides shaved away; *Bevels* have one or more edges rounded off; *Suckers* have a concave side that is said to stick to the table. Dice with *Edge Work* are serrated, shaved, or cut in a certain way as to influence the roll – but are too unreliable for most cheats, and can easily be spotted by others. *Electric dice* with one metallic face were used with magnetic playing surfaces. Casinos that cheated in this way became known as *juice joints*.

Since *c.*1400BC the opposing sides of six-sided dice have add up to seven in the following manner: 6 faces 1; 5 faces 2; 4 faces 3. Consequently, the most unsubtle of all *gaffed* die are those that are simply misspotted in some way. Generically, such dice are known as *Horses*, *Ts*, or *Busters*, though there are a variety of sub-categories: *Tops & Bottoms*, which will never roll craps; *Door Pops*, which will roll 7 or 11 on every roll; and so on. Misspotted *High Number* and *Low Number* dice are often employed with games like backgammon where high rolls are most useful. When the *mittman* introduces a *gaffed* dice or die into a game (a technique known as *ripping*) those in on the scam can often identify the false die *(brick)* by glancing at the face of the 3 which is often spotted in such a way as to identify it to those in the know. In C16th England rigged dice were known as *Gourds* or *Fulhams* after the louche London suburb notorious for blacklegs and dice cheats. If rigged to throw high numbers (5–12) they were known as *High Fulhams* or *Gourds*; if 1–4 they were known as *Low Fulhams* or *Gourds*. As Shakespeare wrote in *The Merry Wives of Windsor*:

> Let vultures gripe thy guts!
> For gourd and fullam holds
> And 'high' and 'low' beguile
> the rich and poor.

―――――――― THE SECOND AMENDMENT ――――――――

'A well regulated militia, being necessary to the security of a free state, the right of the people to keep and bear arms, shall not be infringed.'

THE BRADY CAMPAIGN
It is doubtful that the Founding Fathers envisioned a time when over 30,000 people are dying from gun violence a year … The vast majority of the American people support reasonable gun control laws and view them as necessary to reduce the level of gun violence in this country. The framers of the Constitution would surely agree.

NATIONAL RIFLE ASSOCIATION
The revolutionary experience caused our forebears to address … the need for the people to maintain a citizen-militia for national and state defense without adopting the bane of liberty, a large standing army. An armed citizenry instead of a standing army was viewed as preventing the possibility of an arbitrary or tyrannical government.

―――――― STEAMBOAT RACES vs HORSE RACES ――――――

During the mid-C19th, steamboat racing flourished on the Mississippi as steamboats set out to prove their speed and thus advertise their services.

I think that much the most enjoyable of all races is a steamboat race; but, next to that, I prefer the gay and joyous mule-rush. Two red-hot steamboats raging along, neck-and-neck, straining every nerve – that is to say, every rivet in the boiler – quaking and shaking and groaning from stem to stern, spouting white steam from the pipes, pouring black smoke from the chimneys, raining down sparks, parting the river into long breaks of hissing foam – this is sport that makes a body's very liver curl with enjoyment. A horse-race is pretty tame and colorless in comparison. Still, a horse-race might be well enough, in its way, perhaps, if it were not for the tiresome false starts. But then, nobody is ever killed. At least, nobody was ever killed when I was at a horse-race. They have been crippled, it is true; but this is little to the purpose.

― MARK TWAIN, *Life on the Mississippi*, 1883

Perhaps the most famous Mississippi steamboat race was also one of the last. In June 1870 John W. Cannon, captain of the *Robert E Lee*, challenged T. P. Leathers, captain of the *Natchez*, to race from New Orleans to St Louis. By stripping the *Robert E. Lee* of cargo and passengers, and by refueling ship-to-ship while under-steam, Cannon beat his rival by several hours, completing the journey in 3 days, 18 hours, 14 minutes.

THE SOCIAL HIERARCHY OF FALCONRY

Falconry was one of the oldest activities to be called the Sport of Kings (see p.140) – and from its introduction into Britain (see p.23) the sport has been tightly woven into the fabric of the country's class hierarchy. In her idiosyncratic 1486 *Book of St Albans*, Dame Juliana Berners presents a hierarchy of hawks and the social ranks with which they were appropriate:

The EAGLE, VULTURE, or MERLOUN for an EMPEROR
The GER-FALCON for a KING
The FALCON GENTLE for a PRINCE
The FALCON OF THE ROCK for a DUKE
The FALCON PEREGRINE for an EARL
The BUSTARD for a BARON
The SACRE for a KNIGHT
The LANER for an ESQUIRE
The MARYLON for a LADY
The HOBBY for a young MAN
The GOS-HAWK for a YEOMAN
The TERCEL for a POOR MAN
The SPARROW-HAWK for a PRIEST
The MUSKET for a HOLY WATER CLERK
The KESTREL for a KNAVE

NHL HOCKEY STICK SPECIFICATIONS

GOALKEEPER		SKATER	
Length	*unlimited*	Length	≤63"
Length of blade	≤15½"	Length of blade	≤12½"
Width of blade	≤3½"	Width of blade	≤3" · ≥2"
Curvature	*unlimited*	Curvature	≤½"
Widened shaft length	≤26"		
Widened shaft width	≤3½"	All sticks must be made of wood	
Width of blade at heel	≤4½"	(or any NHL approved material)	
Knob	≥½"	but may be reinforced with tape.	

Played between two mathematics teachers, Adolf Anderssen and Lionel Kieseritzky, at the Chess Divan at Simpson's-in-the-Strand in 1851, the 'Immortal' Game has become one of the most famous battles of chess (even though some question the merit of this fame). In his day Anderssen was considered to be one of the world's strongest tournament players and his daring sacrifice of a bishop, two rooks, and his queen to force checkmate was seen as both creative and bold. Wilhelm Steinitz declared: 'in this game there occurs almost a continuity of brilliancies, every one of which bears the stamp of intuitive genius, that could have been little assisted by calculations, as the combination-point arises only at the very end of the game.' Ernst Falkbeer gave the match its nickname in 1855, though actual immortality has been guaranteed in a number of ways. In 1984 Surinam issued a 90¢ stamp with a layout of the board after the 20th move; a version of the endgame is played between Sebastian and Tyrell in Ridley Scott's 1982 film *Blade Runner*; and since 1923 the townsfolk of Marostica in Italy have played out the game on a life-size board with real human players.

Anderssen [white] · Kieseritzky [black]

1 ... e4	...... e5	13 .. h5	...... Qg5
2 .. f4	...... exf4	14 .. Qf3	..... Ng8
3 .. Bc4	... Qh4+	15 .. Bxf4	.... Qf6
4 ... Kf1	...... b5	16 .. Nc3	..... Bc5
5 ... Bxb5	.... Nf6	17 .. Nd5	... Qxb2
6 ... Nf3	..... Qh6	18 .. Bd6	... Bxg1
7 .. d3	...... Nh5	19 .. e5	... Qxa1+
8 .. Nh4	.... Qg5	20 .. Ke2	.... Na6
9 .. Nf5	...... c6	21 .. Nxg7+	.. Kd8
10 .. g4	...... Nf6	22 .. Qf6+	... Nxf6
11 .. Rg1	.... cxb5	23 .. Be7#	 1-0
12 . h4	...... Qg6	*See p.80 for notation.*	

Curiously, sources differ in their account of the moves, and some assert that Kieseritzky actually resigned after the 20th move. The diagram below shows the final state of the board after Anderssen achieved mate in the 23rd move:

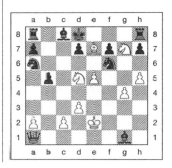

———————————— IDLE WORMS ————————————

It used to be said that little worms ('idle worms') bred in the fingers of indolent servants, to which Shakespeare alludes in *Romeo & Juliet* [I. iv.]:

'A round little worm Pricked from the lazy finger of a maid'

─────── CHEATING & GAMESMANSHIP ───────

TONYA HARDING plotted to have her rival Nancy Kerrigan nobbled by an assailant before the 1994 US National Skating Championships.

ROSIE RUIZ was the first woman to finish the Boston Marathon in 1980 – after joining the race just half a mile from the end. (Ruiz had only qualified for the Boston race after a fast time in New York when she had taken the subway.) Ruiz may have been inspired by FRED LORZ, who won the 1904 St Louis Olympics marathon by 'running' 11 miles as a passenger in a car.

THE SPANISH INTELLECTUALLY DISABLED BASKETBALL TEAM won paralympic Gold in 2000. However, it transpired that 10 of the 12 team members had no intellectual disability whatsoever.

An age-old scam of golf cheats is 'inch creeping', where players edge their balls nearer to the hole when they mark them on the green. In 1985, a Scottish professional was banned from playing as a pro for 20 years by the PGA for 'inch creeping' his ball up to 20 feet.

In the Tintin adventure *Flight 714*, the millionaire who never laughs, LASZLO CARREIDAS, cheats at a game of battleships with Captain Haddock. Carreidas uses CCTV aboard his private jet to spy on the Captain's board – however, he gets his comeuppance as the airplane is hijacked and Carreidas never gets to finish the game.

WILLIAM WEBB ELLIS, a pupil of Rugby school, is usually (if almost certainly erroneously†) credited with creating the game of rugby in 1832 when, cheating during a game of football, he picked up the ball and ran with it. The school commemorates this act, calling it 'fine disregard for the rules'. However, young William was described by a contemporary as 'one who was inclined to take unfair advantages at football'.

†Considerable doubt surrounds this story, not least because it seems never to have been told by Webb Ellis himself. Instead, it was recounted by an old Rugbeian, Matthew Holbeche Bloxam, some fifty years after the event. Notwithstanding this, many similar games existed prior to William's cheating, including *Harpastum* – a Roman game that involved both scrummaging and the carrying of the ball.

In Ian Fleming's novel *Goldfinger*, AURIC GOLDFINDGER cheats at cards and golf. James Bond oufoxes him both times – on the golf-course by switching Auric's Dunlop 65 No.1 for a No.7: 'Too bad we were playing to the rules. Afraid that means you lose the hole. And, of course, the match.'

STELLA WALSH set twenty world records, won Gold in the 100m in the 1932 Olympics, and was inducted into the US Track and Field Hall of Fame. However, an autopsy after her murder revealed that Walsh suffered from the rare genetic disease Mosaicism, which endowed 'her' with male genitals and chromosomes of both sexes.

During the Ashes tour of 1932–3 the England captain Douglas Jardine employed the controversial BODYLINE bowling technique (known also as 'leg theory') in an attempt to contain the devastating talent of Australian batsman Don Bradman. Pace bowlers such as Harold Larwood and Bill Voce were instructed to pitch short, fast balls directly at the batsman's body – a tactic that left the Australians the unenviable choice of being hit by the ball or risking an easy catch to the phalanx of fielders Jardine had placed short on the leg side. While England's tactics fell short of actual cheating, they were condemned by many as the nadir of unsporting play. Australia's captain Bill Woodfull said 'there are two teams out there. One is trying to play cricket'. In contrast, when Larwood's fast bowling felled Woodfull with a blow to the heart, Captain Jardine quipped, 'Well bowled, Harold!' In response to 'leg theory' the rules of cricket were changed to limit the number of fielders behind square leg.

DIEGO MARADONA blatantly scored a 52nd-minute goal against England in the 1986 World Cup with his hand. He later claimed: 'It was partly the hand of Maradona and partly the hand of God'.

BORIS ONISCHENKO, fencing in the 1976 Olympics in Montreal, wired up his épée so that he could trigger the electronic scoring system at will.

In the 1970s and 1980s EAST GERMANY suddenly began to rival the USA & USSR in the medals stakes. It emerged that in their desperation to prove Eastern superiority, the state authorities had sponsored drug taking, telling the athletes they were vitamins.

During the 1978 *Tour de France*, cyclist MICHEL POLLENTIER used a system of rubber tubing to provide a fake urine sample. This foreshadowed Danny's invention of 'a device enabling the drunken driver to operate in absolute safety' described in the film *Withnail & I*. The 1998 *Tour de France* was dubbed the *Tour de Dopage*, after 234 doses of the drug EPO were found in a Festina team's car.

Eight members of the CHICAGO WHITE SOX baseball team were charged with 'throwing' the 1919 World Series in return for huge bribes from a gang of gamblers. A number of players confessed, including 'Shoeless' Joe Jackson, and all eight were suspended.

In 1981, when Australia were playing New Zealand in a World Series Cup game at the MCG, New Zealand required six off the final ball to win the match. In an act of supreme gamesmanship, the Aussie captain GREG CHAPPELL instructed his brother Trevor to bowl an underarm 'grubber' along the grass, making it impossible for the New Zealand number ten, Brian McKechnie, to hit a six.

FENCING BLADES & THEIR TARGETS

The FOIL is the modern version of a sword designed to aid dueling practice. It is the lightest of the three weapons. The target area is the torso (both front and back), excluding the head. Valid hits can only be scored with the point of the blade.

The ÉPÉE is the modern version of the dueling rapier, and is the heaviest of the three weapons. The target area is the whole body, and whoever hits first scores a point (if both fighters should make a hit at the same time, both score a point).

The SABRE is the modern version of the cavalry sword, and is designed as a cutting weapon. The target area mirrors that of a horseman, and is anywhere above the waist, including head and arms. Hits are scored with the point or the cutting edges.

weight <500g
blade length 90cm

weight <770g
blade length 90cm

weight <500g
blade length 88cm

SCORING BILLIARDS

Cannon	2	Pot red	3
Pot white	2	In-off red	3
In-off white	2	*If combined in a stroke, all are scored*	

In-offs hit with a cannon score, in addition to the cannon, the following:

If the red was struck first by the cue-ball	3
If the object white was struck first	2
If both object balls were struck simultaneously	2

GAMBLING CRUSADERS

In 1190, Kings Richard I and Philip of France jointly established an edict regulating gambling with games of chance by members of the Christian crusading armies. No person under the rank of KNIGHT was permitted to play any game for money; KNIGHTS and CLERGYMEN could play for stakes lower than 20 shillings per day and night; the MONARCHS could, naturally, play for whatever stakes they chose. but their attendants were restricted to stakes of 20 shillings. If any exceeded this sum, they were to be whipped, naked, through the ranks of the troops for three whole days.

SOME COLLECTORS & THEIR COLLECTIONS

Collector	*Collects*
antiquist	antiques
arctophile	teddy-bears
bibliophile	books
broadsider	broadsides
chiffonier	scraps of fabric
conchologist	shells
copoclephile	key-rings
crabologist	crabs
deltiologist	postcards
discophile	gramophone records
incunabulist	early books
logophile	words
notaphilic	banknotes
numismatist	coins
pasquinader	lampoons, satires
philatelist	stamps
phillumenist	matchbooks
preterist	historical objects
rhapsodist	literary pieces
tatterer	refuse, rags
tegestologist	beer-mats

HONORARY HARLEM GLOBETROTTERS

The following have been awarded the title *Honorary Harlem Globetrotter*:

Jesse Jackson (2000) · Pope John Paul II (2000)
Jackie Joyner-Kersee (1999) · Nelson Mandela (1996)
Whoopi Goldberg (1989) · Kareem Abdul-Jabbar (1989)
Bob Hope (1977) · Henry Kissinger (1976)

OLYMPIC HORSE COLOR NOMENCLATURE

The color codes for horses entered into Olympic equestrian events are:

DU	Dun	PA	Palomina	PB	Piebald
AP	Appaloosa	GR	Gray	LB	Light Bay
BA	Bay	CH	Chestnut	DC	Dark Chestnut
BL	Black	DB	Dark Bay	RO	Roan

—————————— SOME CHESS QUOTATIONS ——————————

WOODY ALLEN · I failed to make chess team because of my height.

BOBBY FISCHER · I like the moment when I break a man's ego.

SHERLOCK HOLMES · Excellence at chess is one mark of a scheming mind.

GEORGE BERNARD SHAW · [chess] is a foolish expedient for making idle people believe they are doing something clever when they are only wasting their time.

TRADITIONAL INDIAN PROVERB Chess is a sea in which a gnat may drink and an elephant may bathe.

LENIN · Chess is the gymnasium of the mind.

JAMIE MURPHY · Chess, like mathematics and music, is a nursery for child prodigies. [*On Budapest's Polgar sisters.*]

THOMAS FULLER · When a man's house is on fire, it's time to break off the chess.

—————————— THE PARALYMPICS ——————————

The Paralympic Games derived from the pioneering work of Sir Ludwig Guttman who, in 1948, organized a competition at Stoke Mandeville for WWII veterans with spinal injuries, asserting that sport aided morale and rehabilitation. By 1960 an global Olympic-style Games had evolved. The aim of the Paralympics is to show athletic victory over disability and, to this end, only the elite may participate. Nowadays, there are 6 categories: spinal cord injury; amputee; visually impaired; cerebral palsy; mentally handicapped; and *les autres* (athletes with motor disability). Disabilities are graded by severity, and individuals compete against those similarly impaired. In 1952, 2 countries and 130 athletes took part; by Sydney 2000, there were 123 countries and 3,843 athletes. In 2001 an agreement between IOC and International Paralympic Committee (IPC) ensured that from 2012 the Olympic host city is obliged to host the Paralympics. Although the IPC asserts that *Paralympic* means 'beside the Olympics', this may be a modern reinterpretation of the word. (The *Oxford English Dictionary* dates 'Paralympic' to 1954, stating it derives from paraplegia: 'paralysis of the lower limbs and a part or the whole of the trunk'.)

—— OLYMPIC SWIMMING POOL SPECIFICATIONS ——

Length	50m	Lane width	2.5m
Width	25m	Water temperature	25°–28°C
Number of lanes	8	Light intensity	>1500 lux

---------------------- ON WALKING ----------------------

❦ To WALK AT ROVER'S is to wander aimlessly with no fixed abode. ❦ As Stern & Stern wrote in their 1992 *Encyclopedia of Pop Culture*, Michael Jackson's signature MOONWALK 'became the single best-known bit of celebrity body language since the four Beatles'. ❦ The notion of the WALKING WOUNDED (i.e. prisoners who could make their own way to the medics) originated during the horrors of WWI. ❦ To WALK THE CHALK is a military and police term for pacing along a chalked line to demonstrate one's (in)sobriety. WALK YOUR CHALK! was an instruction to quit one's lodgings – it might originate from the practice of chalking the doors of houses that were to be requisitioned by the army or monarchy. ❦ SLEEPWALKING (also noctambulation or somnambulism) tends to occur in the deep stages of NREM sleep (see p.88) and tends to last from a few minutes to half-an-hour. During episodes of sleepwalking, individuals are usually able to perform complex motor functions and often have no memory of their actions when they awake. ❦ As *Dire Straits* noted: 'And after all the violence and double talk, There's just a song in all the trouble and the strife, You do the walk, you do the WALK OF LIFE.' ❦ When Australian Aboriginals GO WALKABOUT they return to the bush for a time to escape Westernized life. When members of the Royal Family GO WALKABOUT they leave the comfort of their cars to shake hands with the *hoi polloi*. ❦ A baseball hitter gets a WALK to 1st base if he is pitched four 'balls' or is touched by a pitched ball. ❦ DOBBY'S WALK is the area haunted by a goblin – in the C19th a 'dobbie' was a household sprite or apparition. ❦ When batsmen WALK in cricket, they abandon the crease even before the umpire has given them out. As Brian Close once said: 'A batsman who knows he is out should walk. That is the way we play the game.' ❦ The LAMBETH WALK is a road in South London which was featured in the 1937 musical *Me and My Gal*. The song (*'Any time you're Lambeth way, Any evening, any day, You'll find us all, Doin' the Lambeth walk'*) was accompanied by a strutting, thumb-jerking dance, and the occasional ejaculation of *'Oi!'*. ❦ A C19th dance of African-American origin, the CAKEWALK originated when slaves parodied the 'genteel' manners of their owners. Dancers would promenade the dance floor, improvizing moves, and the most stylish would be awarded a cake. ❦ The Minister of SILLY WALKS (John Cleese) was not at all impressed with Mr Pudey's (Michael Palin's) silly walk: 'It's not particularly silly, is it? I mean, the right leg isn't silly at all and the left leg merely does a forward aerial half turn every alternate step.' ❦ To GO BY WALKER'S BUS, to TAKE THE MARROWBONE STAGE, and to RIDE SHANK'S PONY are all euphemisms for walking. ❦ In shooting parlance, beaters drive or WALK UP to dislodge birds from the undergrowth into the oncoming hail of shot. ❦ To be ordered to WALK SPANISH is to be made redundant, as is to be given one's MARCHING ORDERS or WALKING PAPERS. ❦ [See also p.19 & p.143.] ❦

ON FITNESS & EXERCISE

MARK TWAIN · I have never taken any exercise except sleeping and resting, and I never intend to take any. Exercise is loathsome. And it cannot be any benefit when you are tired; and I was always tired.

ROBERT MAYNARD HUTCHINS · Whenever the urge to exercise comes upon me, I lie down for a while and it passes.

NEIL ARMSTRONG [attrib.] · I believe that every human has a finite number of heart-beats. I don't intend to waste any of mine running around doing exercises.

BARBARA EHRENREICH · Exercise is the yuppie version of bulimia.

HENRY FORD · Exercise is bunk – if you are healthy, you don't need it. If you are sick, you shouldn't take it.

ANNA QUINDLEN · I feel about exercise the same way that I feel about a few other things: that there is nothing wrong with it if it is done in private by consenting adults.

JOHN F. KENNEDY · Our growing softness, our increasing lack of physical fitness, is a menace to our security.

BARRY GRAY · I get my exercise running to the funerals of my friends who exercise.

CALORIE EXPENDITURE

The approximate Calories burnt each minute by those weighing *c.*150lb:

Sitting still.......1–2	Yoga 4–6	Skipping.........7–9
Snooker..........2–6	Dancing 4–6	Tennis 7–9
Walking 2–6	Skipping.........4–7	Morris dancing.7–10
Frisbee...........3–5	Badminton 5–6	Tennis singles ..7–12
Fishing...........3–6	Brisk walking....5–8	Football 7–13
Housework 3–6	Aerobics class....5–9	Basketball 8–11
Golf 3–6	Ping-Pong 6–7	Jogging.........8–13
Cricket 3–7	Water skiing 6–9	Langlauf........8–13
Trampoline 3–9	Sex 6–11	Martial arts.....8–13
Fencing..........4–6	Swimming......6–12	Squash 8–13
Gymnastics 4–6	Ice skating 7–9	Water-polo 8–13

These figures are approximate and will vary depending on a number of factors, from how vigorous the gymnastics to the incline of the hill climbed or the weight of the golf clubs carried. For every pound over 150lb, add 10%; for every pound under 150lb, subtract 10%. With a small 'c', a calorie is the amount of energy required to heat 1g of water by 1ºC. With a capital 'C' (a kilocalorie or 1,000 calories) it is the amount of energy required to heat 1kg of water by 1ºC, or 4.2kJ. [Sadly, 1 chocolate éclair = *c.*190 Calories.]

CURLING

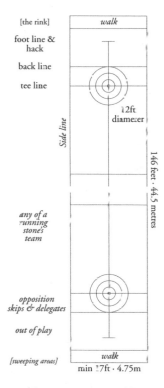

[the rink] — walk

foot line & hack

back line

tee line

12ft diameter

Side line

146 feet · 44.5 metres

any of a running stone's team

opposition skips & delegates

out of play

[sweeping areas] — walk

min 17ft · 4.75m

Curling originated in Scotland, where it was played on frozen ponds. Like an icy version of bowls, two teams of four compete in the best of eight 'ends'. The object of each end is to place as many stones within the scoring area, using strategy to try and ensure your team scores the most, whilst expelling or blocking your opponents' stones from the 'house'. Curling's most conspicuous quirk is the use of brooms to sweep before the curling stones. This splendidly domestic activity serves to stop the stones bending and speeds their flight.

SOME CURLING TERMS

Rink .... *a curling team*
Skip .... *captain of the team*
House .... *name of the scoring area*
Eight-ender ...... *a perfect end when every stone scores a point*
End .... *a round*
Bonspiel ...... *a curling tournament*
Button .... *the center of the target*
Gripper .... *ridged curling shoe*
Slider .... *smooth curling shoe*
Hurry .... *encouragement to sweepers*

A curling team consists of four players who throw two stones (or rocks) in turn – alternating with the opposition players. The other players on the team act as sweepers. The *lead* throws the 1st & 2nd stones, setting up play, and then sweeps for the next 6. The *second* throws the 3rd & 4th, aiming to take out the other team's stones. The *third* (also known as *vice* or *mate*), throws the 5th & 6th rocks, aiming to set the stage for the *skip* or *captain*, who throws remaining stones which often prove to be vital.

Shot number	who throws	who sweeps
1 & 2	Lead	Second & Third
3 & 4	Second	Lead & Third
5 & 6	Third	Lead & Second
7 & 8	Skip	Lead & Second

—————————— SATCHEL'S ADVICE ——————————

The legendary baseball pitcher Leroy 'Satchel' Paige (1906?–82) was famed as much for his fast wit as his fast balls. He played in over 2,500 games and notched up more than 50 no-hitters. In 1948 Paige was the first black pitcher in the American League, and in 1971 he made history as the first 'Negro League' player to be inducted into the Baseball Hall of Fame. He printed the following advice to fans on the back of his autograph cards:

'Six Rules For A Happy Life'
Avoid fried meats which angry up the blood.
If your stomach disputes you, lie down and pacify it with cool thoughts.
Keep the juices flowing by jangling around gently as you move.
Go very lightly on vices such as carrying on
in society. The social ramble ain't restful.
Avoid running at all times.
Don't look back. Something may be gaining on you.

Woody Allen was such a fan of Paige that he named son (with Mia Farrow) Satchel. The son Allen and Farrow adopted was named after the talented NBA player Moses Malone.

—————————— ROCK, PAPER, SCISSORS ——————————

The origin of the classic game of ROCK, PAPER, SCISSORS has been the subject of much debate. It is possible that a version of the game may have been played by Roman soldiers, who used WATER, FIRE, WOOD (water extinguishes fire, which burns wood, which floats on water). However, no record of the hand signals has been discovered. The Japanese call the game *Jan-ken-poh* or *Janken* – and they use it as a method to choose the dealer in card games, who will serve first at tennis, and so on. (*Hasami* is scissors; *kami* is paper; *ishi* is stone.) Some versions of the game employ four possible hand shapes. For example, French schoolchildren nowadays play with ROCK *(caillou)*, WELL *(puits)*, PAPER *(feuille)*, and SCISSORS *(sciseaux)*. Here, scissors fall down the well, which is covered by paper, which is cut by scissors, which are smashed by rock, which also falls down the well. And, there is an ancient Abyssinian variation with eight signs: needle, sword, scissors, hammer, Imperial razor, sea, altar, and the sky.

—————————— BOOKMAKER'S WISDOM ——————————

If you back favorites, you'll have no laces in your boots.
If you back outsiders, you'll have no boots.

— JOE *'King of the Ring'* THOMPSON, bookmaker, *c.*1860

—BACKGAMMON BOARD LAYOUT & TERMS—

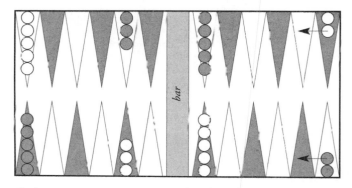

Backgammon	a game won when the loser has *borne off* no *men* and still has *men* on the *bar* or in the winner's *home board*
Bearing off	removing *men* from the board
Blank	an unplayable roll of the dice
Blot	a *point* occupied by a single *man* vulnerable to a *hit*
Comeback	when a *man* on the *bar enters* and *hits* a *blot*
Crossover	a move across the *bar*
Doublet	a throw of doubles
Enter	to move a *man* off the *bar*
Gammon	a game won when the loser has *borne off* no *men*
Hit	an attack on a *blot*, sending the man to the *bar*
Home table	the side of the board in which the game ends
Making a point	placing two or more *men* on a *point*
Man	a piece
Outer table	the opposite half to the *home table*
Point	one of the 24 triangles
Taking up	removing a *man* from a *blot*
Turn the cube	to offer a double (see below)

When backgammon is played for money, the *doubling cube* may be used to increase the stakes. At any stage before a player has rolled the dice to start a turn, their opponent may offer to continue the game at double the initial stakes – assuming that no double has previously been proposed. If the player accepts (*takes*) the wager the stakes are increased and that player *owns* the *doubling cube* and enjoys the option to propose future doubles. (The *ownership* of the cube alternates depending on who has accepted the last double.) If a player declines (*drops* or *passes*) a double they concede the game and the stakes. The cube itself is marked 2, 4, 8, 16, 32, and 64, and is placed on the *bar* to show the current betting level.

─────── TEN-PIN BOWLING SPLITS & TERMS ───────

A SPLIT is the combination of pins left standing after the first throw, assuming the first throw has knocked over at least one pin† but not all of them (which is known as a STRIKE). A range of terms exists to describe the various possible SPLITS, which vary in difficulty depending on the amount of space between the remaining pins. (SPLITS are called in numerical order.)

Nickname of split	*pins standing after first ball*
BABY *or* MURPHY	2/7 *or* 3/10
BACK ROW	7/8/9/10
BED POSTS *or* GOAL POSTS *or* SNAKE EYES	7/10
BIG FOUR *or* DOUBLE PINOCHLE	4/6/7/10
BIG THREE	1/2/3
BUCKET	2/4/5/8 *or* 3/5/6/9
CHRISTMAS TREE *or* FAITH, HOPE, CHARITY	3/7/10 *or* 2/7/10
CINCINNATI	8/10
CLOTHESLINE *or* PICKET FENCE *or* RAIL	1/2/4/7 *or* 1/3/6/10
DIME STORE	5/10
POISON IVY	3/6/10
SLEEPERS	2/8 *or* 3/9
SOUR APPLE *or* LILLY	5/7/10
STRIKE SPLIT	8/10 *or* 7/9

† If the first ball leaves the headpin standing, the remaining balls cannot be termed a split. So, the combinations 1/2/10, 1/2/4/10, 1/3/7, 1/3/6/7, &c., are known as WASHOUTS.

In addition to these split nicknames, bowling has a wealth of other terms:

Anchor . *last man on a team to roll*	Moat . . . . *slang for the gutter*
Balsa . . *weak strike on the head pin*	Mother-in-law . . . . *the 7 pin*
Bicycle. . . . *a pin hidden by another*	Nose. . . . *hitting the headpin full on*
Box. . . . . *a single frame*	Nothing . . . . *a no-score ball*
Cherry. . . . . . . *taking the front pins*	Open. *frame with no strike or spare*
Creeper . . . . *a slow ball*	Pie alley . . . . *a forgiving lane*
Dodo . . . . *an illegal ball*	Pinching . . . . *over-gripping the ball*
Double . . . . *2 strikes in a row*	Pocket. . . . *space between 1/3 or 1/2*
Five bagger . . . . . . *5 strikes in a row*	Poodle. . . . . *a gutter ball*
Foundation . . . . . *a 9th-frame strike*	Sixpack. . . . . *6 strikes in a row*
Four bagger . . . . . *4 strikes in a row*	Sleeper . . . . *a hidden rear pin*
Graveyards . . . . *low-scoring lanes*	Strike out . . *3 strikes in 10th frame*
Headpin . . . . [usually] *the 1 pin*	Tandem. . . *a pin hidden by another*
Honey. . . . . *a sweet roll*	Tap . . . . . . *to leave one pin standing*
Kingpin . . . . [usually] *the 5 pin*	Turkey. . . . . *3 strikes in a row*

There are any number of versions of the playground game 'it', all of which are based on the premise that one player is 'it' – and 'it' is very contagious.

SAFETY · where players are safe if they are touching an agreed object. However, only one person can touch the object at any time.

JOIN ME · where any player who is touched by 'it' becomes 'it' *as well*. The last uninfected player wins.

CONGA · players who are touched by 'it' must clasp 'it' around the waist and join them in their pursuit. In this way, an 'it' conga-line forms; but only the first and last in the line can 'it' another.

BALL · best played in an enclosed space: 'it' is armed with a tennis or football, and 'it' is transferred to the first player that the ball touches. Clearly, 'it' must carefully judge the violence of their throws.

STATUES · an agreed number of the pursued are deemed statues, who are immune from 'it' but must remain motionless. Others can seek respite from the chase by tapping a statue on the shoulder and swapping places, at which time the former statue is fair game.

STICK IN MUD · a player who is touched by 'it' becomes stuck in a star-jump position, and can only be unstuck from the mud by another player crawling through their legs. If 'it' manages to stick all the players in the mud, the last player to be stuck becomes 'it'.

OFF THE GROUND · Players are safe from 'it' if both of their feet are off the ground; manhole covers count, but jumping does not.

———————————————— POKER CHAMPIONS ————————————————

The roll-call of Champions from the legendary *World Series of Poker*:

'70........*Johnny Moss*	'82 ....*Jack Straus*	'94 ..... *Russ Hamilton*
'71.... . .*Johnny Moss*	'83....... *Tom McEvoy*	'95 ... *Dan Harrington*
'72.. . .*Amarillo Slim*[†]	'84 ....*Jack Keller*	'96 .... *Huck Seed*
'73.. ... *Puggy Pearson*	'85..........*Bill Smith*	'97 ....*Stu Ungar*
'74........*Johnny Moss*	'86 ..... *Berry Johnston*	'98...... *Scotty Nguyen*
'75 ...... *Sailor Roberts*	'87.......*Johnny Chan*	'99....... *Noel Furlong*
'76 ..... *Doyle Brunson*	'88.......*Johnny Chan*	'00 ..... *Chris Ferguson*
'77 .. ..*Doyle Brunson*	'89...*Phil Hellmuth Jr*	'01... *Carlos Mortensen*
'78 .... *Bobby Baldwin*	'90. *Mansour Matloubi*	'02.... *Robert Varkonyi*
'79.........*Hal Fowler*	'91.. ..*Brad Daugherty*	'03. *Chris Moneymaker*
'80 ....*Stu Ungar*	'92 *Hamid Datsmalchi*	'04....... *Greg Raymer*
'81 ....*Stu Ungar*	'93 ....*Jim Bechtel*	[† AKA *Thomas Preston*]

—————————— FORMULA ONE FLAGS ——————————

Checkered . . . . *race has finished*
Red . . . . *race has been stopped for safety reasons*
Blue . . . . *a faster car is behind and trying to lap a backmarker*
White . . . . *warns of a slow-moving vehicle (e.g. safety car)*
Red & yellow striped . . . . *track slippery (e.g. due to water or oil)*
Yellow . . . . *danger ahead; overtaking prohibited*
single yellow wave . . . . *slow down*
double yellow wave . . . . *drivers must be prepared to stop*
Orange disc on black (with number) . . . . *indicates that a car must stop in*
pits immediately because of a mechanical fault
Black & white diagonals (with number) . . . . *warning for unsportsmanlike*
behavior (may be followed by a black flag)
Black (with number) . . . . *driver must stop in pits immediately*
usually to be disqualified for breaking the rules
Green . . . . *hazard cleared; cars can race as normal*

—————————— HOPSCOTCH ——————————

Hopscotch is a playground game played all around the world, with a wide variety of different grids and local rules. The most basic version of the game involves players taking it in turns to throw a flat stone into the first box of a grid. They then hop up and down the grid until they retrieve their stone. Players can place their feet where they like on the undivided areas (e.g. 4), but must straddle the divided areas (e.g. 2 & 3). If a player completes a run without standing on a line or stumbling, they can throw their stone to the next square, and repeat the process. (Variations include: kicking the stone from box to box as you hop; claiming and initialing with chalk a personal square that no other player can land on; or completing the board with a stone balanced variously on your head, foot, or hand.) For years it has been claimed that hopscotch dates to Roman times, when centurions would apparently use the game for fitness training as they traveled up and down the roads to and from the capital. Iona and Peter Opie, the authorities on childhood games, pour scorn on this notion, dating hopscotch to the mid-C17th. However, the myth might explain why 'London' is often chalked on the final turning square.

————— TAROT CARD INTERPRETATIONS —————

The Tarot pack consists of 78 cards: 22 picture cards of the *major arcana* and 56 suited cards of the *minor arcana* – and it is likely that these two arcana originally formed separate packs. Debate surrounds the oldest known Tarot pack – some claim the 1415 pack belonging to the Duke of Milan, others the 1392 pack made for Charles VI. Even more debate surrounds the origin, symbolism, design, and interpretation of the cards, which have for centuries been used by mystics, soothsayers, fortune tellers, and charlatans. One interpretation of the *major arcana* is below:

Common interpretation	MAJOR ARCANA	Interpretation if reversed
Important decisions needed	FOOL	*problems from reckless actions*
Strength of will and initiative	MAGICIAN	*failure of nerve; hiding from reality*
Influence & insight of wise woman	PAPESS	*risk of emotional instability*
Fertility, motherhood, protection	EMPRESS	*domestic upheaval; male weakness*
Self-control; power; knowledge	EMPEROR	*immaturity; failed ambition*
Good advice; teaching	POPE	*misinformation, poor advice*
Time of choice; intuition	LOVERS	*danger of moral lapse, indecision*
Victory through effort; triumph	CHARIOT	*overbearing influence, ruthlessness*
Agreement through negotiation	JUSTICE	*partisanship, bias, ill judgment*
The need to slowly plan and think	HERMIT	*refusal to heed good advice*
Start of a new cycle; regeneration	WHEEL	*turn for the worse; good cycle ends*
Courage to take a risk	FORTITUDE	*defeat; failure of nerve*
Wisdom; mental agility	HANGED MAN	*materialism; inner struggle*
Major change (often for good)	DEATH	*the element of chance*
Deft handling of circumstances	TEMPERANCE	*progress thwarted by foolishness*
Hidden forces at work	DEVIL	*lust for or abuse of power*
Capricious suffering; disaster	TOWER	*unnecessary suffering*
Insight; widening horizons	STAR	*rigidity of a closed, narrow mind*
Crisis of faith	MOON	*failure of nerve*
Success against the odds	SUN	*misjudgment ending in failure*
Accomplishment; new beginnings	JUDGMENT	*wasted opportunities; loss; guilt*
Successful completion of matters	WORLD	*stagnation; inertia; no momentum*

It is claimed that these cards correspond to the 22 letters of the Hebrew alphabet, each with complex numerological and Kabbalistic significance. The cards of the *minor arcana* are grouped into four suits: cups, swords, coins, and staves (or wands), which are said to represent clergy, nobility, merchants, and peasants. Each suit consists of number cards from one to ten and four court cards: King, Queen, Knave, and Knight (see also p.139). Perhaps the most famous fictional Tarot readers are Madam Sosostris who has 'a wicked pack of cards' in T.S. Eliot's 1922 epic *The Wasteland*, and Solitaire (Jayne Seymour) in the Bond film *Live & Let Die* (1973). When James Bond picks out the Fool, Solitaire smirks 'You have found yourself.'

——CURIOUS SPORTING ACTIVITIES OF NOTE——

LA TOMATINA takes place on the last Wednesday of August (the peak of tomato season) in the Spanish village of Buñol. For two hours more than 90,000 pounds of tomatoes are indiscriminately hurled at everything and everyone by 30,000 or so revellers. It seems this annual food-fight began by accident in the 1940s when a friendly meal got out of hand.

EXTREME IRONING, according to its advocates, combines 'the thrills of an extreme outdoor activity with the satisfaction of a well pressed shirt'. The prerequisites are a hot iron, a challenging physical environment (in oncoming traffic, under water, on a mountainside), a bundle of creased clothing, and perhaps a little starch.

The 22-mile MAN *vs* HORSE RACE has been run in Wales since 1979, when Screaming Lord Sutch was the official starter. In June 2004 it was won by a human for the very first time in 2 hours, 5 min, 9 secs.

Britain's annual CHEESE ROLLING contest takes place each May down Cooper's Hill, near Brockworth in the Gloucestershire Cotswolds. A 7–8lb Double Gloucester cheese is released from the top of the hill, and participants scramble down the precipitous bank (which has gradients of 1:2 and 1:1) in a vain attempt to catch it. Four races are held (one for women) and, in each case, the first to the foot of the hill wins the cheese.

Twice a year on Christmas Day and New Year's Day the men and boys of Kirkwall (on the Mainland of Orkney) play the KIRKWALL BA'. Traditionally, the two teams were formed by accident of birth: those born north of St Magnus Cathedral are *Doonies* (Doon-the-Gates), those born south are *Uppies* (Up-the-Gates). The BA' is a handmade leather ball filled with cork which, on the stroke of 1pm, is tossed into the assembled crowd from the Mercat Cross in front of the Cathedral. Both teams attempt to get the ball and carry it through the streets to their goals: the *Uppies* try to touch the BA' against a wall in the south of the town; the *Doonies* try to get it into the water of the harbor to the north.

BUZKASHI – the Afghan national sport – translates literally as 'goat grabbing', and for good reason. A headless, hoofless, and eviscerated goat carcass (the *boz*) is placed in the center of a circle, and two opposing teams on horseback attempt to seize it and carry it to the goal area. [The sport is featured in John Frankenheimer's 1971 film classic *The Horsemen*, starring Omar Sharif.]

The Colombian sport TEJO is akin to the traditional games of deck quoits or horseshoes except that it involves high explosives. Players attempt to toss a ball, disc, or stone into a target area which contains a series of blasting caps *(totes)*. The player who causes most explosions is deemed the winner.

— CURIOUS SPORTING ACTIVITIES OF NOTE cont. —

On the second Sunday of August, LA POURCAILHADE takes place in the French pig-raising town of Trie-sur-Baïse. The festival is dedicated to all things porcine, but the highlight is the 'pig squealing competition' where contestants mimic the sounds that pigs make in a variety of real-life scenarios: eating, copulating, giving birth, facing the butcher, and so on.

The OMAK SUICIDE RACE has been run each August since 1935 in Omak, Washington. A 120-foot run-in prepares the 20 or so riders and horses for the 210-foot descent (with a gradient of 62º), at the bottom of which flows the Okanogan River. However, as the number of horses injured or killed has increased, so has the vocal opposition to the race.

Other curious activities of note include the WORLD GURNING CONTEST held each year as part of the Egremont Crab Apple Fayre in Cumbria, UK, where participants compete to pull the most hideous faces; the Welsh BOG SNORKELING CHAMPIONSHIPS where competitors wade though 60 yards of putrid bog-water; Finland's justly famous WIFE-CARRYING championship where husbands carry their wives over a 253·5m obstacle course in order to win their spouse's weight in ale; the Polish WORLD SCREAMING CHAMPIONSHIP held in Goldap; and the MOSQUITO KILLING CHAMPIONSHIP held in Pelkosenniemi, Finland, where the 1995 record of 21 mosquitos killed in 5mins stands.

———— POKER HANDS & PROBABILITIES ————

1,098,240 ways	One pair	35 to 24
123,552 ways	Two pairs	20 to 1
54,912 ways	Three of a Kind	46 to 1
10,200 ways	Straight	254 to 1
5,108 ways	Flush	508 to 1
3,744 ways	Full House	693 to 1
624 ways	Four of a Kind	4,164 to 1
36 ways	Straight Flush	72,192 to 1
4 ways	Royal Flush	649,739 to 1

———————— MUSCLE ————————

40–50% of the human body consists of muscle – contractile tissue which is able to initiate or sustain movement. Three basic types of muscle exist:

SKELETAL .. *under voluntary control; usually attatched to bone via tendons*
SMOOTH . *not under voluntary control; occurs in the gut, blood vessels, &c.*
CARDIAC .... *occurs only in the heart; beats rhythmically*

—————————— PARLOR GAME FORFEITS ——————————

Some forfeits which may be usefully employed with the games on pp.20–1:

COMPLIMENTS · The victim must pay each of the assembled company a heartfelt compliment.

PERFORM THE PARROT · The victim must ask each person, 'If I were a parrot, what would you teach me to say?', and then has to repeat what they are instructed. If a woman instructs a man to say 'Who's a pretty boy then?' the man is obliged to kiss her.

ACT THE SULLEN MUTE · The victim must perform whatever tasks they are instructed without speaking, laughing, or smiling.

CONTRADICTION · For a period of time, the victim must perform the opposite of whatever they are instructed by the company.

MAKING A WILL · The victim must apportion one of their belongings to each member of the company (presumably in a manner which is not legally binding).

TRUTH OR DARE · The victim must answer any question with complete candor, or perform a dare (which may be another of the forfeits here listed).

COURTESY · The victim must go around the room and kneel to the most witty, bow to the prettiest, and kiss the one they love best.

MOODY ROOM · The victim must laugh in one corner of the room, sing in another, cry in another, and dance in the last.

TEMPERANCE · The victim must abstain from alcohol for a period of time (a most serious forfeit).

AGONY AUNT · The victim must go round the room and proffer a piece of advice to all present.

ANIMAL MAGIC · The victim must ask each person in the room what their favorite animal is and do an impression of each.

—————————— SOME EQUINE NOMENCLATURE ——————————

Colt	male, aged 4 and under, not castrated, not mated with a mare
Dam	a horse's mother
Filly	female up to the age of 4
Gelding	castrated male
Juvenile	2-year-old [flat racing]; 3- or 4-year-old [jumps]
Maiden	a horse yet to win a race
Mare	female 4 or older *or* any female that has been bred
Sire	a horse's father
Stallion	male that mates with mares

——————— SOME MARBLES OF NOTE ———————

Aggies.. *marbles fabricated from agate*
Alleys .... *marbles fabricated from alabaster*
Bumboozers .... *extra large marbles*
Cat's eyes......................... *clear marbles with a twist of color inside*
Chinas.................................... .. *marbles fabricated from china*
Clearies.. *clear glass marbles of a single color*
Commies......................... *common marbles, fabricated from clay*
Milkies................................... .... *opaque, milky-white marbles*
Onion skins................... .... *colored marbles, decorated with swirls*
Peewees .... *small marbles*
Sulfides .... *valuable marbles of clear glass with clay figures inside*

Marbles can also be employed as a remedy for snoring. Simply sew a marble into the collar of the snorer's nightshirt, and they will be discouraged from sleeping on their backs.

——————— BUMPER-STICKER INNUENDO ———————

A selection of bumper-sticker slogans advocated by sporting enthusiasts:

· ANGLERS do it in their wellies · ARCHERS do it with a quiver · BOXING PROMOTERS do it for the money · BRIDGE PLAYERS do it with a rubber · CARD SHARPS do it with sleight of hand · CHESS players do it all for the King · CLIMBERS do it up against the wall · CRESTA riders do it head first, face-down · CROQUET PLAYERS do it before they peg out · DARTS players do it on the oche · DECATHLETES do it over two days · DIVERS do it under pressure · DRAUGHTS PLAYERS do it with a huff · FENCERS do it with protection · FISHERMEN do it with their flies down · GAMBLERS do it until they go bust · GLIDERS keep it up all day · GOLFERS do it with an interlocking grip · HOCKEY PLAYERS do it with an Indian dribble · JOCKEYS do it with a whip · JUGGLERS do it with balls · KNIFE THROWERS do it with glamorous assistants · MOUNTAINEERS do it with crampons · PING-PONG PLAYERS do it with spin · POKER PLAYERS do it with a straight face · POT-HOLERS do it in the dark · RACING DRIVERS do it in pole position · RALLY NAVIGATORS do it with tulips · REFEREES do it with a whistle · RUGBY players do it with odd-shaped balls · SCRABBLE PLAYERS do it up and down · SKIERS do it on the piste · SNOOKER players need a long rest · SNORKELERS do it without coming up for air · SPIN BOWLERS do it with a Chinaman · SWIMMERS go to great lengths to do it · TENNIS players do it from love · TRAMPOLINISTS do it in the air · WALKERS do it with their feet on the ground · WATER SKIERS do it on the pull · WEIGHTLIFTERS do it with a clean snatch · WINDSURFERS do it standing up · YACHTSWOMEN do it with buoys ·

CROQUET IN AMERICA

During the 1860s croquet swept across the Atlantic into America, where it was immediately embraced by most as a truly elegant and fashionable sport and, above all, a great civilizer. The New York periodical *Galaxy* declared in 1867 that 'croquet is an essentially social game, provocative of good humour, wit and fellowship, one in which old men forget their gout, young ones their bills unpaid; in which old ladies trip gayly across the sod in the chase of an 'enemy' ... in which the young ones blend duty and enjoyment so evenly that health blooms in their cheeks, lustre in their eyes, and renewed life throbs in every elastic step'. One manual of croquet went even further, claiming that croquet was 'a protection from evil influences by keeping all members in the household ranks ... [since] with rational amusements at home, no-one will be inclined to seek irrational ones abroad'. Yet not all were so enamoured. In 1878, the *American Christian Review* listed the inevitable disastrous consequences of social activities such as croquet (see diagram). In 1867, the Commissioners of New York's Central Park made a generous exception to their normal prohibition of active adult sports. Splendidly, they allowed young girls to play croquet in secluded areas – away from main thoroughfares – on Wednesday and Friday afternoons.

a social party
social & party play
croquet party
picnic & croquet party
picnic, croquet, & dance
absence from church
imprudent or immoral conduct
exclusion from the church
a runaway match
poverty & discontent
shame & disgrace
ruin

TOUR DE FRANCE JERSEY COLORS

Jersey color	Introduced	Awarded for
Yellow	1919	overall fastest time
Green	1953	most points
White & red polka-dot	1975	best climber
White	1975	best young rider ($\leq$25)

The Yellow Jersey is so colored because the original race sponsor – the newspaper *L'Auto* – was printed on yellow paper. The red and white shirt owes its origin to the sponsor Poulain chocolates; and the green shirt to the gardening shop Belle Jardinier. Between 1984 and 1988 a red jersey was awarded to the leader of the intermediate sprint bonus competition. A Competitiveness Prize is awarded at each stage to the rider who has made the most effort and has demonstrated the best sportsmanship. The Competitiveness Prize winner for each particular stage wears special blue number bibs for the following stage; and the most aggressive and combative rider in each stage wears special red number bibs.

INTERNATIONAL PLAYING CARD PACKS

Pack	Suits	Court cards	Numerals	Standard deck
GERMAN	leaves, acorns, hearts, bells	King, Over, Under	7, 8, 9, 10, Ace	32
SWISS	shields, acorns, flowers, bells	King, Over, Under	6, 7, 8, 9, 10, Deuce	36
SPANISH	swords, clubs, cups, coins	King, Knight, Valet	1, 2, 3, 4, 5, 6, 7	40
ITALIAN	swords, batons, cups, coins	King, Knight, Footsoldier	1, 2, 3, 4, 5, 6, 7	40
FRENCH	spades, clubs, hearts, diamonds	King, Queen, Knave	Ace, 2, 3, 4, 5, 6, 7, 8, 9, 10	52

ELY CULBERTSON · A deck of cards [is] built like the purest of hierarchies, with every card a master to those below it, a lackey to those above it. ❧ ALEXANDER POPE · See how the world its veterans rewards! A youth of frolics, an old age of cards. ❧ SAMUEL JOHNSON · I am sorry I have not learned to play at cards. It is very useful in life: it generates kindness and consolidates society.

ATHLONS

Biathlon	skiing, shooting
Triathlon (standard)	swimming 3-8km, cycling 180km, marathon run 42.195km
Terrathlon	riding, shooting, swimming, running
Quadrathlon	(usually) running, swimming, cycling, and canoeing.
Pentathlon (traditional)	jump, javelin throw, 200m race, discus throw, 1500m flat race
Pentathlon (modern)	showjumping, fencing, pistol shooting, 200m swim, 3,000m cross-country run
Pentathlon (women)	shot put, high jump, 100m hurdles, 800m race, long jump
Pentathlon (ancient)	running (c.200yds), long jump, discus, javelin, wrestling
Heptathlon (women)	[day 1] 100m hurdles, shot put, high jump, 200m race; [day 2] long jump, javelin, 800m race
Decathlon	[day 1] 100m, long jump, shot put, high jump, 400m; [day 2] 110m hurdles, discus, pole vault, javelin, 1,500m

—— THE SPORT OF KINGS & OTHER NICKNAMES ——

The Sport of Kings[1] .... horse racing
The Noble Art[2] .... boxing
The Gentle Craft[3] .... angling
The Beautiful Game[4] .... soccer
The Noble Science of Defence .... fencing
The Tesserarian Art[5] .... gambling

[1] The Sport of Kings has been the nickname for a number of activities – some more sporting than others. In the C17th the term was a euphemism for WAR. Later, perhaps through belligerent associations with cavalry horses, the term was applied to HUNTING, although FALCONRY also enjoyed similar royal associations. Nowadays HORSE RACING and occasionally POLO are the sports most commonly linked with the phrase. Curiously, SURFING was dubbed the Sport of Kings as early as 1935, at least according to an article of that year in the magazine *Hawaiian Surfboard*. It seems that this unlikely association arose because surfing was traditionally the exclusive recreation of the Hawaiian royal family. TEN-PIN BOWLING's claim to be the Sport of Kings probably rests on the first (or middle) pin, which is known as the kingpin (see p.130). Riders of the CRESTA RUN (see p.53) consider their pursuit the King of Winter Sports. [2] In addition to BOXING, the Noble Art has also been associated with SELF-DEFENCE, KITE FLYING, BILBOQUET (cup-and-ball), and THIMBLERIGGERY (sleight-of-hand contricks). [3] It has been suggested that this nickname might be a pun on the word 'gentle' – a term for the maggots (the larvae of the flesh-fly or bluebottle) which were traditionally employed by anglers as bait. Izaak Walton (1593–1683), author of *The Compleat Angler*, a classic pastoral account of fishing, was bestowed the monicker 'The Gentle'. Angling should of course not be confused with the Gentle Art of Persuasion or, indeed, the *Gentle Art of Making Enemies*, 1890, by James McNeill Whistler. [4] Dutch soccer player Ruud Gullit extended the notion of the Beautiful Game by coining the phrase 'sexy football' to describe his vision of the game. This is not to be confused with the other Dutch notion of 'total football' popularized in the 1970s, that advocated an all-rounder approach to player skills and positions. PELOTA (or JAI ALAI) has on occasion been called the Beautiful Game. [5] An archaic term which derives from the Latin for dice: *tesserae* (see p.116).

—— HANDKERCHIEFS AND BULLFIGHTS ——

In the language of bullfighting the *pañuelo* is a handkerchief used by the *presidente* (adjudicator) of the fight to signal his orders. A WHITE *pañuelo* is used to signal the start of the parade; the release of the bulls; and the various stages of the fight. And, once the bull is dead, one wave of the WHITE *pañuelo* signals the *matador* will be awarded one ear; two waves signals both ears; three waves signals both ears and the tail. A GREEN *pañuelo* signals that the bull is to be returned to the corrals because it is defective or because it cannot be killed. A RED *pañuelo* signals that larger *banderillas* (spiked sticks) must be used to coax a recalcitrant bull to charge – an act which brings disgrace both to the bull and its breeder.

—— COMPARATIVE BALL SIZE SCHEMATIC ——

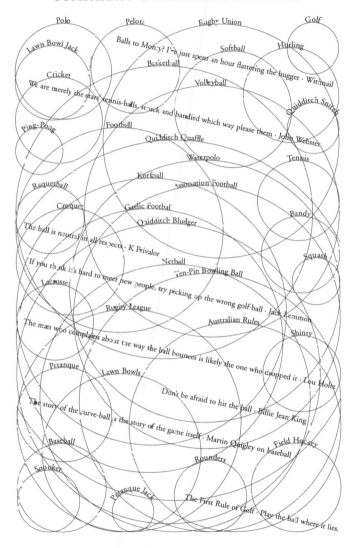

Polo
Pelota
Rugby Union
Golf
Lawn Bowl Jack
Balls to Money? I've just spent an hour flattering the bugger · Withnail
Softball
Hurling
Cricket
Basketball
We are merely the stars tennis-balls, struck and bandied which way please them · John Webster
Volleyball
Ping-Pong
Football
Quidditch Snitch
Quidditch Quaffle
Waterpolo
John Webster
Korball
Tennis
Racquetball
Association Football
Croquet
Gaelic Football
Bandy
Quidditch Bludger
The ball is neutral in all respects · K Privalor
Netball
Squash
If you think it's hard to meet new people, try picking up the wrong golf ball · Jack Lemmon
Lacrosse
Ten-Pin Bowling Ball
Rugby League
Australian Rules
The man who complains about the way the ball bounces is likely the one who dropped it · Lou Holtz
Shinty
Petanque
Lawn Bowls
Don't be afraid to hit the ball · Billie Jean King
The story of the curve-ball is the story of the game itself · Martin Quigley on baseball
Baseball
Field Hockey
Snooker
Rounders
Petanque Jack
The First Rule of Golf · Play the ball where it lies.

The schematic is based on the maximum circumference of the ball. Scale: 1mm ≈ 10mm

——— WORLD SERIES RESULTS ———

It's splendidly English to invent a World Series in which only Americans play.
— WILFRED GOWERS-ROUND

year	winner	loser
2004	Boston 4	St. Louis 0
2003	Florida 4	NY Yankees 2
2002	Anaheim 4	San Francisco 3
2001	Arizona 4	NY Yankees 3
2000	NY Yankees 4	NY Mets 1
1999	NY Yankees 4	Atlanta 0
1998	NY Yankees 4	San Diego 0
1997	Florida 4	Cleveland 3
1996	NY Yankees 4	Atlanta 2
1995	Atlanta 4	Cleveland 2
1994		not held
1993	Toronto 4	Philadelphia 2
1992	Toronto 4	Atlanta 2
1991	Minnesota 4	Atlanta 3
1990	Cincinnati 4	Oakland 0
1989	Oakland 4	San Francisco 0
1988	Los Angeles 4	Oakland 1
1987	Minnesota 4	St. Louis 3
1986	NY Mets 4	Boston 3
1985	Kansas City 4	St. Louis 3
1984	Detroit 4	San Diego 1
1983	Baltimore 4	Philadelphia 1
1982	St. Louis 4	Milwaukee 3
1981	Los Angeles 4	NY Yankees 2
1980	Philadelphia 4	Kansas City 2
1979	Pittsburgh 4	Baltimore 3
1978	NY Yankees 4	Los Angeles 2
1977	NY Yankees 4	Los Angeles 2
1976	Cincinnati 4	NY Yankees 0
1975	Cincinnati 4	Boston 3
1974	Oakland 4	Los Angeles 1
1973	Oakland 4	NY Mets 3
1972	Oakland 4	Cincinnati 3
1971	Pittsburgh 4	Baltimore 3
1970	Baltimore 4	Cincinnati 1
1969	NY Mets 4	Baltimore 1
1968	Detroit 4	St. Louis 3
1967	St. Louis 4	Boston 3
1966	Baltimore 4	Los Angeles 0
1965	Los Angeles 4	Minnesota 3
1964	St. Louis 4	NY Yankees 3
1963	Los Angeles 4	NY Yankees 0
1962	NY Yankees 4	San Francisco 3
1961	NY Yankees 4	Cincinnati 1
1960	Pittsburgh 4	NY Yankees 3
1959	Los Angeles 4	Chicago White Sox 2
1958	NY Yankees 4	Milw. Braves 3
1957	Milw. Braves 4	NY Yankees 3
1956	NY Yankees 4	Brooklyn 3
1955	Brooklyn 4	NY Yankees 3
1954	NY Giants 4	Cleveland 0
1953	NY Yankees 4	Brooklyn 2
1952	NY Yankees 4	Brooklyn 3
1951	NY Yankees 4	NY Giants 2
1950	NY Yankees 4	Philadelphia 0
1949	NY Yankees 4	Brooklyn 1
1948	Cleveland 4	Boston Braves 2
1947	NY Yankees 4	Brooklyn 3
1946	St. Louis 4	Boston Red Sox 3
1945	Detroit 4	Chicago Cubs 3
1944	St Ls. Cardinals 4	St Ls. Browns 2
1943	NY Yankees 4	St Ls. Cardinals 1
1942	St Ls. Cardinals 4	NY Yankees 1
1941	NY Yankees 4	Brooklyn 1
1940	Cincinnati 4	Detroit 3
1939	NY Yankees 4	Cincinnati 0
1938	NY Yankees 4	Chicago Cubs 0
1937	NY Yankees 4	NY Giants 1
1936	NY Yankees 4	NY Giants 2
1935	Detroit 4	Chicago Cubs 2
1934	St. Louis Cardinals 4	Detroit 3
1933	NY Giants 4	Washington 1
1932	NY Yankees 4	Chicago Cubs 0
1931	St Ls. Cardinals 4	Phild. A's 3
1930	Phild. A's 4	St. Louis Cardinals 2
1929	Phild. A's 4	Chicago Cubs 1
1928	NY Yankees 4	St Ls. Cardinals 0
1927	NY Yankees 4	Pittsburgh 0
1926	St Ls. Cardinals 4	NY Yankees 3
1925	Pittsburgh 4	Washington 3
1924	Washington 4	NY Giants 3
1923	NY Yankees 4	NY Giants 2
1922	NY Giants 4	NY Yankees 0
1921	NY Giants 5	NY Yankees 3
1920	Cleveland 5	Brooklyn 2
1919	Cincinnati 5	Chicago White Sox 3
1918	Boston Red Sox 4	Chicago Cubs 2
1917	Chicago White Sox 4	NY Giants 2
1916	Boston Red Sox 4	Brooklyn 1
1915	Boston Red Sox 4	Phil. Phillies 1
1914	Boston Braves 4	Philadelphia As 0
1913	Philadelphia As 4	NY Giants 1
1912	Boston Red Sox 4	NY Giants 3
1911	Philadelphia As 4	NY Giants 2
1910	Philadelphia As 4	Chicago Cubs 1
1909	Pittsburgh 4	Detroit 3
1908	Chicago Cubs 4	Detroit 1
1907	Chicago Cubs 4	Detroit 0
1906	Chicago W. Sox 4	Chicago Cubs 2
1905	NY Giants 4	Philadelphia As 1
1904		not held
1903	Boston Red Sox 5	Pittsburgh 3

Baseball is an allegorical play about America, a poetic, complex, and subtle play of courage, fear, good luck, mistakes, patience about fate, and sober self-esteem.
— SAUL STEINBERG

──────── ROCKY'S FIGHTS ────────

Sylvester Stallone wrote all five *Rocky* films himself after being inspired by a fight between 'nobody' Chuck Wepner and Muhammad Ali, in which Wepner, to everyone's astonishment, lasted the full fifteen rounds.

MOVIE	OPPONENT	OUTCOME
Rocky (1976)	Apollo Creed[1]	*Creed wins on split decision – 15R*
Rocky II (1979)	Apollo Creed	*Rocky wins – KO 15R*
Rocky III (1982)	Clubber Lang[2]	*Rocky loses – KO 2R*
		rematch; Rocky wins – KO 3R
Rocky IV (1985)	Ivan Drago[3]	*Rocky wins – KO 15R*
Rocky V (1990)	Tommy Gunn[4]	*Rocky defeats the punk in a street fight*

The first *Rocky* film won the Academy Award for Best Picture (beating *All The President's Men* and *Taxi Driver*) and Sylvester Stallone himself was nominated for Best Actor. [1] Apollo Creed was played by Carl Weathers. [2] Clubber Lang was played by the legendary Mr T. During the film he utters the immortal line *'No, I don't hate Balboa … I pity the fool!'.* [3] Ivan Drago was played by Dolph Lundgren. *Rocky IV* portrays a Cold War grudge match prompted by Russian Ivan Drago killing American Apollo Creed. After beating Drago, Rocky makes a toe-curling anti-Cold War speech, to encourage friendship and understanding between the two countries. [4] Tommy Gunn was played by Tommy 'the Duke' Morrison.

──────── NAISMITH'S RULE ────────

W.W. Naismith, a founder of the Scottish Mountaineering Club, devised a formula to enable walkers in hilly or mountainous regions to estimate the time required for an expedition. The premise of Naismith's Rule was to allow one hour for every 5km (3 miles) measured on the map plus an additional half-hour for every 300m (1,000ft) ascended. For example:

10km (∴ 2h) on map + 870m (∴ 1½h) climb = 3½ hours

Naturally this formula assumes reasonable fitness, good weather, a group of equal speed, good conditions underfoot, and a bearable weight of pack. Most consider Naismith to have been either remarkably bullish or just plain optimistic, and many expeditions cautiously add 50% extra time. A host of other walkers (Aitken, Tranter, Langmuir, Kennedy, et al.) have proposed more sophisticated methods of calculation that take into account such factors as type of terrain underfoot, speed of descent, seasonal variations, headwind, fatigue, weather conditions, and so on.

GLADIATORS

Unique to Roman culture, gladiators originated at funerals (in *c.*264BC) when combat displays replaced sacrifices. The popularity of the grim and bloody gladiatorial games became such a part of Roman life that in AD326 Constantine felt the need to suppress them. The gladiators themselves were criminals, slaves, or prisoners of war, and most did not survive for very long. Occasionally, victorious fighters developed a certain fame, earning money, gifts, and visits from women. However, their ultimate goal was to receive the *rudis* – a wooden sword which conferred freedom. A variety of gladiators fought against each other (as well as wild animals):

Andabata · 'Blind-fighters' who wore full helmets with no eye-holes; their challenge was to fight using their remaining senses.

Secutor · 'Chasers', they carried a dagger and wore only a helmet, metal guards on the left leg, and padding on the sword arm.

Eques · Fought on horseback with a 2-meter-long lance and sword. They wore helmets and had fabric wrappings on their lower legs.

Retiarius · Lightly armed and mobile, they wore no helmet and only their sword arm and shoulder were protected. They were armed with a net and trident.

Samnite · Took their name from a tribe defeated by the Romans in 312BC. They wore plumed helmets, carried large oblong shields, and fought with a sword.

Provocator · Known as challengers, they wore helmets with visors and breast-plates, and carried round shields and straight-edged swords.

Myrmillo · 'Fish man' – so called due to a distinctive fin-like crest on their helmets. They were equipped with a large shield and fought with a sword.

Hoplomachus · Heavily armored with metal guards on their lower legs and fabric wrapping on their thighs and sword arm. They fought with a lance and dagger.

Thracian · Fought with a short curved sword and wore a wide-brimmed helmet with crest.

Bestiarii · The lowest-ranking gladiators, they fought wild beasts with only whips or spears.

Debate rages over the role of the thumb in gladiatorial arenas since no conclusive pictorial evidence has been unearthed. It seems that when a gladiator fell he would appeal to the mercy of the crowd with a raised index finger. Most sources agree that, in response, the crowd would either 'press the thumb' or 'turn the thumb', but it is unclear what these meant. It is often claimed that an upturned thumb meant death and a downturned thumb life – though the opposite explanation is to be found in many sources. In Ridley Scott's *Gladiator* (2000) an upturned thumb signified life and vice versa. Here, the life of Gladiator Maximus (Russell Crowe) is spared when the crowd chant 'save' and make a thumbs-up gesture, thus compelling Emperor Commodus to spare the life of his enemy.

— DRAG RACE CATEGORIES & CHRISTMAS TREES —

Drag racing is a straight-line contest of raw acceleration between two vehicles over a measured distance – usually ¼ mile (1,320'), or ⅛ mile (660'). A vast array of classes and categories exist (which differ between race organizers), but there are four basic classes of professional drag cars:

TOP FUEL · the ultimate cars for drag racing, they can travel from a standing start to 100mph in under a second. They are fueled by nitromethane, of which they can burn 15 gallons (*c.*$500) each race.

FUNNY CAR · supercharged cars fueled by methanol or ethanol and clad in fiberglass or carbon fiber. They can travel ¼ mile in 5·7 seconds at over 240mph.

PRO STOCK · two-door coupé or sedan street cars, less than 5 years old, with gas-burning carburetor engines that can generate over 200mph. Because of its link with production cars, pro-stock class is considered a purist's category.

PRO MODIFIED · a diverse class of vehicles with modified engines and chassis, some with supercharging or nitrous oxide injection.

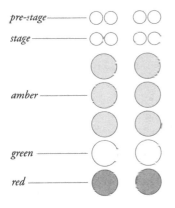

Races are started and timed by lights called the 'Christmas tree'. When an infrared beam about 9" from the start-line is broken the *pre-stage* lights are lit. A second beam on the start-line triggers the *stage* lights when the front of the tyre breaks it. (When the front tyre crosses this beam, the car's time starts.) The three *amber* lights illuminate together to indicate that the race is about to begin, and 0·4 seconds later the *green* go light is lit. If cars cross the line before *green,* the *red* foul light comes on.

———— HOURS REQUIRED FOR SLEEP ————

A *traveler* five hours doth crave,
To sleep, a *student* seven will have,
And nine sleeps every idle *knave*.

or

Nature requires six · *Custom* seven · *Laziness* nine · and *Wickedness* eleven

—— CLASSIFICATION OF 'BLIND' SPORTSMEN ——

In an attempt to prevent cheating and to ensure fair competition, disabled and impaired sporting organizations employ medical tests to assess the degree of impairment of sportsmen and women. For example, by measuring an athlete's best eye at its highest possible correction, the International Blind Sports Federation (IBSF) classifies the blind and visually impaired into the following four groups:

[NOE] · Not eligible; a visual acuity over 6/60 and/or visual field of more than 20 degrees.

[B3] · From a visual acuity of above 2/60 to a visual acuity of 6/60 and/or a visual field or more than 5 degrees and less than 20 degrees.

[B2] · From the ability to recognize the form of a hand to a visual acuity of 2/60 and/or a visual field of less than 5 degrees.

[B1] · Total absence of perception of the light in both eyes, or some perception of the light but with inability to recognize the form of a hand at any distance and in any direction.

———————— CORINTHIANS ————————

In addition to delineating an ornate order of Greek columns, the term Corinthian is used in the world of sport to describe a keen, often wealthy, usually fashionable, amateur. From at least the C16th, Corinthian had a pejorative sense and was used to damn a class of idle and utterly shameless fornicators. To Shakespeare, the Corinthian was a 'fast man' or 'blood':

'I am no proud Jack, like Falstaff; but a Corinthian,
a lad of mettle, a good boy.' – *I Henry IV*, II:iv

Francis Grose, in his 1785 *Dictionary of the Vulgar Tongue*, describes Corinthians as 'frequenters of brothels; also an impudent brazen faced fellow'. It seems these associations derived from the louche behavior popularly held to be endemic in Greek and Roman Corinth. Over time, the term became less harsh and it was used to describe both fashionable 'swells' and dilettante sportsmen. Nowadays, a number of amateur sports teams dub themselves Corinthians, though in the United States, Corinthianism tends to be largely associated with the sport of yachting.

———————— ARROBAS ————————

Arrobas are the units used to weigh fighting bulls in Spain. 1 *arroba* is roughly equal to 25lbs; the ideal weight for a bull is said to be 30 *arrobas*.

DEATH & LAUGHTER

CHALCHAS · A soothsayer who died laughing at the thought that he had outlived the time he predicted for his own death.

ZEUXIS · The C5thBC painter who died laughing at the sight of an old hag whom he had just painted.

PHILOMENES · Died laughing at the sight of an ass eating his figs.

MARGUTTE · A giant who died of laughter watching a monkey trying to put on a pair of boots.

TOMMY COOPER · True giant of comedy who died on-stage to the sound of laughter, 15 April 1984.

CRASSUS · Died from laughing on seeing an ass eat thistles.

MRS FITZHERBERT · Died on 19 April 1782 at the Drury Lane Theatre while laughing at the poor performance of an actor.

For details of the Burmese king who died laughing, see p.50 of *Schott's Original Miscellany.*

TANGRAM PUZZLES

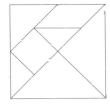

The Tangram or Anchor Enigma is a traditional Chinese puzzle that consists of a square dissected into seven shapes: five triangles, a square, and a rhombus. (The Chinese name *Ch'i ch'iao t'u* translates as 'seven ingenious plan'.) Several hundred shapes can be made from these pieces (all of which have to be used), but some of the most complex are those that seem the simplest:

[For the solution to these classic tangram puzzles, turn to p.160.]

ON RUNNING & AGE

Running races should be absolutely forbidden to men over 27 years of age. Between 30 and 40, a man may indulge in running at a moderate pace for exercise, but not in races. Men over 60 years of age should never run at all for anything, not even to catch a train.

— JAMES CANTLIE, *Physical Efficiency*, 1906

———————— ON DREAMS AND DREAMING ————————

CARL JUNG · Your vision will become clear only when you can look into your own heart ... Who looks outside, dreams; who looks inside, awakes.

RALPH WALDO EMERSON · Judge of your natural character by what you do in your dreams.

JOAN DIDION · We all have the same dreams.

WILLIAM DEMENT · Dreaming permits each and every one of us to be quietly and safely insane every night of our lives.

SADIE DELANY · In our dreams, we are always young.

W.B. YEATS · I have spread my dreams under your feet. Tread softly because you tread on my dreams.

HENRY DAVID THOREAU · If one advances confidently in the direction of his dreams, and endeavors to live the life which he has imagined, he will meet with a success unexpected in common hours.

HENRIK IBSEN · Castles in the air – they're so easy to take refuge in. So easy to build, too.

WILLIAM SHAKESPEARE · We are such stuff As dreams are made on; and our little life Is rounded with a sleep.
[*The Tempest*, IV.i.]

STEPHEN VINCENT BENÉT · Dreaming men are haunted men.

BOB DYLAN · I am against nature. I don't dig nature at all. I think nature is very unnatural. I think the truly natural things are dreams, which nature can't touch with decay.

CHUANG TSE · I do not know whether I was then a man dreaming I was a butterfly, or whether I am now a butterfly dreaming I am a man.

FRIEDRICH NIETZSCHE · I fly in dreams, I know it is my privilege, I do not recall a single situation in dreams when I was unable to fly. To execute every sort of curve and angle with a light impulse, a flying mathematics – that is so distinct a happiness that it has permanently suffused my basic sense of happiness.

GEORGE BERNARD SHAW · You see things; and you say Why? But I dream things that never were; and I say Why not?

JOHN UPDIKE · Dreams come true; without that possibility, nature would not incite us to have them.

GÉRARD DE NERVAL · Dreams are a second life. I have never been able to penetrate without a shudder those ivory or horned gates which separate us from the invisible world.

——— ON DREAMS AND DREAMING cont. ———

MARCEL PROUST · If a little dreaming is dangerous, the cure for it is not to dream less but to dream more, to dream all the time.

VICTOR HUGO · To substitute day-dreaming for thought is to confuse a poison with a source of nourishment.

STEPHEN BROOK · Unpinned even by rudimentary notions of time and space, dreams float or flash by, leaving in their wake trails of unease, hopes, fears and anxieties.

T.E. LAWRENCE · All men dream: but not equally. Those who dream by night in the dusty recesses of their minds wake in the day to find that it was vanity: but the dreamers of the day are dangerous men, for they may act their dream with open eyes, to make it possible.

ERICH FROMM · Both dreams and myths are important communications from ourselves to ourselves. If we do not understand the language in which they are written, we miss a great deal of what we know and tell ourselves in those hours when we are not busy manipulating the outside world.

MICHEL DE MONTAIGNE · I hold that it is true that dreams are faithful interpreters of our drives; but there is an art to sorting and understanding them.

VIRGINIA WOOLF · Yet it is in our idleness, in our dreams, that the submerged truth sometimes comes to the top.

SIGMUND FREUD · Interpretation of dreams is the royal road to a knowledge of the unconscious activities of the mind. (See p.77.)

——— CHOOSING 'it' ———

Many playground games, not least 'it' (see p.131), use elaborate procedures to select the 'infected' child. Apart from rock, paper, scissors (see p.128), a range of rhymes or 'dips' are employed to determine the odd one out:

Eeny meeny macker racker
Rare ie domi nacker
Chicker bocker lolli popper
Om pom push

Hurcum, borcum,
curious corkum,
Harricum, berricum, buzz;
Eggs, butter, cheese, bread,
Stick, stock, stone dead.
[AMERICAN]

Red, white and blue
The cat's got the flu
The dog's got chicken pox,
So out goes YOU!

El el, eopéné,
Sevoux sooya sagsama,
Gidén Haléb yolena;
Haléb dedi guin Pazar.
Haidé boona check boune
[ARMENIAN]

One potato, two potato,
Three potato, four
Five potato, six potato
Seven potato, more!

Your shoes are dirty,
Your shoes are clean,
Your shoes are not fit
To be seen by the Queen.

'Ekkero, akai-ri, you, kair-an
Filiussin, follasy, Nicholas ja'n
Kivi, kavi, Irishman,
Stini, Stani, buck.
[ROMANY]

Ickery, ahry, oary, ah,
Biddy, barber, oary, sah,
Peer, peer, mizter, meer,
Pit, pat, out, one.

Ichiku, tachikio, tayemosaro,
otoshime, samaga, cniugara,
mo, ni, owarite, kikeba,
hoho, hara, no kai.
[JAPANESE]

———————— A FATHER'S ADVICE TO HIS SON ————————

Mark Hanbury Beaufoy (1854–1922), MP for Kennington (1889–95), wrote these lines for his eldest son, Henry Mark Beaufoy, on giving him a gun:

If a sportsman true you'd be, Listen carefully to me:

Never, never let your gun
Pointed be at anyone;
That it may unloaded be
Matters not the least to me.

When a hedge or fence you cross,
Though of time it cause a loss,
From your gun the cartridge take,
For the greater safety's sake.

If twixt you and neighbouring gun,
Birds may fly or beasts may run
Let this maxim e'er be thine:
Follow not across the line.

Stops and beaters oft unseen
Lurk behind some leafy screen;
Calm and steady always be:
Never shoot where you can't see.

Keep your place and silent be:
Game can hear and game can see;
Don't be greedy, better spared
Is a pheasant than one shared.

You may kill or you may miss,
But at all times think of this:
All the pheasants ever bred
Won't repay for one man dead.

———————————————— NIM ————————————————

Although the game probably originated in China – where it is known as *Tsyanshidzi* – Nim was named and popularized in 1901 by mathematician C.L. Bouton, who used it to explore binary. Nim is a deceptively simple game for two that can be played with any set of similar objects from cards or matches to pebbles or coins. (The game's name derives from the German *nehmen* – to take.) The objects are laid as opposite, and the players take turns in removing any number of objects they like *from one row only.* The player who removes the last object is the loser (or winner, depending on which version is played). The most stylish game of Nim is that played in Alain Resnais' 1962 film *L'année dernière à Marienbad*, which has the following dialogue: 'I know a game I always win.' – 'If you can't lose, it's no game.' – 'I can lose, but I always win.'

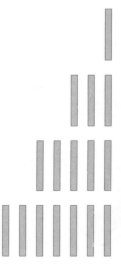

———BALLROOM DANCING TIMES & TEMPOS———

dance	time	tempo
Waltz	3/4	bpm 30
Foxtrot	4/4	30
Quickstep	4/4	52
Tango	2/4	33
Viennese Waltz	3/4	60

Rumba	4/4	27
Samba	2/4	52
Cha Cha Cha	4/4	32
Paso Doble	2/4	62
Jive	4/4	44

[International Dancesport Federation]

———TUGS OF WAR ROPE SPECIFICATION———

As defined by The Tug of War International Federation:
The rope must not be less than 10 centimeters (100 mm), or more than 12·5 centimetres (125 mm) in circumference, and must be free from knots or other holdings for the hands. The ends of the rope shall have a whipping finish. The minimum length of the rope must not be less than 33·5 meters.

——— PULLING THE GOOSE & CLUBBING THE CAT ———

In C17th New York, PULLING THE GOOSE was a regular Shrove Tuesday tradition. A live goose was procured, its neck was generously lubricated with soap, oil, or other unguents and it was suspended from rope tied between two stakes. Contestants on horseback then took it in turn to gallop at full pelt towards the goose, attempting to rip off the bird's head as they passed A variant of this sport involved a live goose that had been suspended from rope over a river or canal. Contestants would stand up in boats, rowed swiftly under the rope, and attempt to rip off the goose's neck as they passed – without falling into the water. (Hares and cats were also used.)

CLUBBING THE CAT usually took place on the green in front of an inn or tavern. A live cat would be placed in a barrel which would then be strung-up off the ground along a length of sturdy rope. Participants, usually well-oiled at the bar, would take it in turn to hurl heavy clubs at the barrel with the intention of breaking the cask and allowing the cat to escape. (Often the cat, traumatized by the violence inflicted upon it, would simply fall to the ground dazed after the barrel had been smashed.) Once the cat had been released from the barrel, it was chased and killed – a bottle of wine was the killer's prize. (Geese and peacocks were also used.)

Both of these sports were generally prohibited by law (for example, Stuyvesant banned pulling the goose on 25 January 1658 – and at the same time prohibited the playing of tennis during church service hours.) On 26 February 1654, Gÿsbert Theunissen van Banevelt was found guilty of pulling the goose and ordered to pay 3 guilders to the poor.

--- THE A.B.C. OF ROWING ---

A is for ACTION,
which must be easily done.

B is for BOAT,
which smoothly must run.

C is for CREW,
who together must row.

D is for DASH,
which makes the boat go.

E is for EASE,
the hallmark of pace.

F is for FEET,
made to make the boat race.

G is for GATHER,
on your stretcher to strike.

H is for HAND,
to draw as you like.

I is that IDOL,
perfect form ever more.

J is that JOKER,
the 'body form' oar.

K is for KICKING,
the stretcher like Hell.

L is for LISTEN:
the boat runs well.

M is the MAXIM
which lies under all:
'If you can't do it easy –
you can't do it at all.'

N is for NEATNESS,
not flashiness or show.

O is for OAR, which
you must learn to row.

P is for POISE:
the foundation of Time.

Q is for QUICKNESS,
to which you must climb.

R is for RING,
the bell note sublime.

S is for SPRING,
if elastic 'twill do.

T is for TIMING,
must be mechanically true.

U is for USE,
the oar as a friend.

V is for VIGOR,
which to victory will tend.

W is for WATER,
one drives with a hit.

X is for EXCELLENCE,
strive ever for it.

Y is for YEARS,
through which you attain,
perfection by rowing,
again and again.

Z is for ZEBRA,
whose stripes represented
by your blade in the water
will make you contented.

Attributed to the
Australian rowing coach
Steve Fairburn, ?1904.

—— A HIERARCHY OF ACTION AND INACTION ——

A host of Victorian writers were preoccupied with the dangers both of an idleness and overactivity. Below is one of many guides to a 'decent' life:

† DEATH †	VIGOR	PASSIVITY
CONVULSION	EAGERNESS	INDIFFERENCE
MANIA	VIM	ATARAXIA
FRENZY	ENTHUSIASM	FALLOWNESS
APOPLEXY	INDUSTRIOUSNESS	APATHY
MAELSTROM	ACTIVITY	SHIFTLESSNESS
TUMULT	LABOR	AIMLESSNESS
TURMOIL	EMPLOYMENT	DORMANCY
ANXIETY	DUTY	FIXITY
HYPERACTIVITY	PRAYER	DESULTORINESS
UPSET		LAZINESS
DISCOMPOSURE	THE BALANCED LIFE OF A HUMBLE	IDLENESS
PERTURBATION	AND DEVOTED PENITENT ·	INDOLENCE
AGITATION	G	INERTIA
EXCITATION	GOD	SLUGGARDNESS
NERVOUSNESS	D	CUNCTATIVE
DISCOMFITURE		INATTENTION
UNQUIETNESS	PRAYER	TORPOR
BUSTLE	SERENITY	AESTIVATION
HUSTLE	TRANQUILITY	NUMBNESS
FIDGETINESS	EQUIPOISE	STAGNANCY
CLUTTER	PLACIDITY	OSSIFICATION
CROWDEDNESS	CONTEMPLATION	VEGETATION
BOTHERATION	QUIETISM	INSENSIBILITY
AMBITION	QUIESCENCE	UNCONSCIOUSNESS
ANIMATION	PHLEGMATICISM	COMA
VIVACITY	IMPERTURBABILITY	† DEATH †

--------------------------------- INDEX ---------------------------------

'Make a long arm, Watson, and see what V has to say.' I leaned back and
took down the great index volume to which he referred. Holmes balanced
it on his knee, and his eyes moved slowly and lovingly over the record of
old cases, mixed with the accumulated information of a lifetime. 'Voyage
of the *Gloria Scott*,' he read. 'That was a bad business ... Victor Lynch the
forger. Venomous lizard or gila. Remarkable case, that! Vittoria, the circus
belle. Vanderbilt and the Yeggman. Vipers. Vigor, the Hammersmith
wonder. Hullo! Hullo! Good old index. You can't beat it. Listen to this,
Watson. Vampirism in Hungary. And again, Vampires in Transylvania.'

— ARTHUR CONAN DOYLE, *The Adventure of the Sussex Vampire*, 1924

—— A.B.C. OF ROWING – BOULE, BUTTOCKS, &C ——

† *The chess term for a position where any move is disadvantageous.*

What readers ask nowadays in a book is that it should improve, instruct, and elevate. This book wouldn't elevate a cow. I cannot conscientiously recommend it for any useful purposes whatever. All I can suggest is that when you get tired of reading 'the best hundred books' you may take this up for half an hour. It will be a change.

— JEROME K. JEROME, *Idle Thoughts of an Idle Fellow*, 1886

——— PROPORTION OF ENTRY TYPES ———

Sporting 48% · Gaming 22% · Idling 30%

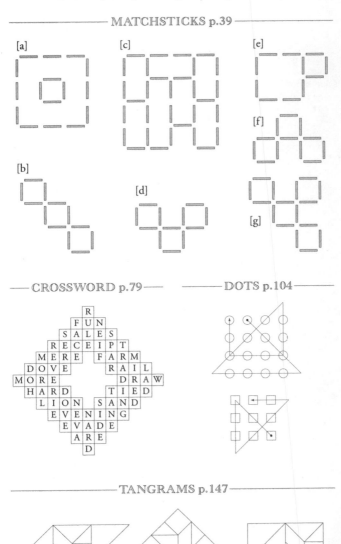

—————————— MATCHSTICKS p.39 ——————————

[a]   [c]   [e]

[f]

[b]   [d]

[g]

—— CROSSWORD p.79 ——   —— DOTS p.104 ——

———————————— TANGRAMS p.147 ————————————